AMERICAN BOYS' LIFE
OF
THEODORE ROOSEVELT

COLONEL ROOSEVELT AT SAN JUAN HILL

AMERICAN BOYS' LIFE
OF

THEODORE ROOSEVELT
BY
EDWARD STRATEMEYER

PREFACE

The life of Theodore Roosevelt is one well worth studying by any American boy who wishes to make something of himself and mount high on the ladder of success.

The twenty-sixth President of our country is a fine type of the true American of to-day, full of vim and vigor, quick to comprehend, and equally quick to act, not afraid to defend his opinions against all comers when satisfied that he is in the right, independent, and yet not lacking in fine social qualities, physically and morally courageous, and with a faith in himself and his God that is bound to make for good so long as he clings to it.

Theodore Roosevelt comes from countless generations of fighting stock, both in this country and abroad. And yet as a youth the future hero of San Juan Hill was a delicate lad, and many fears were entertained that he might not live to manhood. But life in the open air, with judicious athletic exercise, accomplished wonders, and he became strong and hardy to an astonishing degree.

The boyhood days of the future President were spent in New York City and at the family's country home, Oyster Bay, Long Island. From there he went to Harvard College, from which he graduated with high honors. Still somewhat delicate in health, he travelled in Europe, studied for a short time at Dresden, and took to climbing the Alps and other noted mountains.

His mind had gravitated toward literature, and he was writing a naval history of the War of 1812 when something prompted him to take up politics, and almost before he knew it he was elected a New York State assemblyman. He served in this capacity for three terms, and many are the stories told of how he fought against corruption first, last, and all the time.

The death of his first wife and of his beloved mother were at this time a great blow to him, and leaving his one little daughter with relatives, he struck out for the great West, where, in the Bad Lands, so called, he located as ranchman and hunter, filling in his spare hours by studying and by writing on various outdoor subjects, works which have become decidedly popular, and which show well his gifts as an author and as an observer of nature.

While still in great part a successful ranchman, he ran for mayor of New York and was defeated. He now devoted himself with increased energy to his literary labors until, soon after, he was appointed by President Harrison a member of the Civil Service Commission. He served on this commission with marked ability for six years, when he resigned to become police commissioner of New York City.

Theodore Roosevelt's work as a police commissioner will not be readily forgotten. The whole tone of the service was at once raised, and for the first time in many years the metropolis had "dry" Sundays, when every saloon in the city was tightly closed. This strict compliance with the law made him some enemies, but to these he paid no heed, for he was doing only his duty.

When William McKinley was nominated for the Presidency the first time, Theodore Roosevelt was one of his most enthusiastic supporters. Upon the election of McKinley, John D. Long was appointed Secretary of the Navy and Theodore Roosevelt became the First Assistant Secretary. Ever since writing his naval history the newly appointed assistant had made a close study of naval matters, and now he applied himself with vigor to the duties of his office; and it was primarily through his efforts that when the war with Spain came, our war-ships and our coast defences were in much better condition than they had been at any time previous in our history.

With the outbreak of the war, Theodore Roosevelt resigned. "My duty here is done," he said. "My place is in the field." And without loss of time he and his intimate friend, Dr. Leonard Wood, began the organization of that body of troops which was officially designated as the First United States Volunteer Cavalry, but which speedily became known everywhere as the Rough Riders, a body as unique as the world has ever seen, being made up of men from all over the Union, but principally from four Territories, and including hunters, cowboys, soldiers of fortune, foot-ball and base-ball champions, college graduates, ex-policemen, with American, Irish, Dutch, German, Mexican, and Indian blood in their veins, truly a remarkable collection, but every man and officer strong and hardy, full of courage, a good horseman, and a fine shot.

From the very start, the Rough Riders were anxious to get into the fight, and the opportunity was not long in coming. From Florida the command was transported to Daiquiri, on the southern coast of Cuba, and then began the advance upon the city of Santiago, which brought on the engagement at La Guasima, followed by the thrilling battle of San Juan Hill, in which the Rough Riders distinguished themselves in a manner that will never be forgotten. In the very thickest of this fight was Colonel Roosevelt, urging his men forward to victory, regardless of the shot and shell falling upon all sides. A hero truly, and such heroes are not forgotten.

Upon the close of the war Theodore Roosevelt thought to retire to private life, but this was not to be. Arriving at New York, he was hailed with delight by thousands, and at the next election was made governor of the Empire State. As governor he made friends in both of the leading political parties by his straightforwardness and his sterling honesty. Men might differ with him politically, but they could never accuse him of doing that which he himself did not firmly believe was right.

His term as governor had not yet expired when President McKinley was nominated for a second term. Again the people at large clamored for Roosevelt, and against his earnest protestations he was forced to accept the nomination for the Vice-Presidency. He was elected, and at the proper time took his seat as presiding officer of the Senate.

It was at this time a blow fell upon our nation from which we have scarcely yet recovered. President McKinley was struck down by the cowardly hand of an assassin. The Vice-President was at this time off on one of his favorite outings, but with all possible speed he came back and was sworn in as President. It was a great responsibility, and many feared that great changes in our government might result. But the fears proved groundless. Young as he was, and he is the youngest of all of our Presidents, he took upon himself the duty of carrying out the intentions of his predecessor, and proving to the world once again that, even though a President die, "the government at Washington still lives."

There is another side to the character of our President which must not be overlooked. He is of strong religious convictions and a member of the Dutch Reformed Church. It is seldom that he is given to preaching, but when he does his words have a sincerity that proves much for the foundation of his character. He stands for what is honest and upright in political and private life, and although, being but human, he may make mistakes, he remains a Chief Magistrate well deserving the highest honors our nation can bestow.

EDWARD STRATEMEYER.

MAY 2, 1904.

CHAPTER I

BIRTHPLACE AND ANCESTRY OF THEODORE ROOSEVELT HIS FATHER'S PHILANTHROPY CITY AND COUNTRY HOME DAYS AT SCHOOL RELIGIOUS TRAINING

"Our country calls not for the life of ease, but for the life of strenuous endeavor. The twentieth century looms before us big with the fate of many nations. If we stand idly by, if we seek merely swollen, slothful ease and ignoble peace, if we shrink from the hard contests where men must win at hazard of their lives and at the risk of all they hold dear, then the bolder and stronger peoples will pass us by and will win for themselves the domination of the world. Let us therefore boldly face the life of strife, resolute to do our duty well and manfully; resolute to uphold righteousness by deed and by word; resolute to be both honest and brave, to serve high ideals, yet to use practical methods. Above all, let us not shrink from strife, moral or physical, within or without the nation, provided that we are certain that the strife is justified; for it is only through strife, through hard and dangerous endeavor, that we shall ultimately win the goal of true national greatness."

These words, taken from President Roosevelt's remarkable speech on "The Strenuous Life," show well the character of the man, his lofty ideals, his sterling courage, his absolute honesty, and unwavering patriotism. He is a typical American in the best sense of the word, and his life is worthy of careful study. From it American boys of to-day, and in generations to come, may gain lessons that will do them much good.

Theodore Roosevelt, the twenty-sixth President of our country, was born in New York City, October 27, 1858. The place of his birth was the old family mansion at 28 East Twentieth Street, in a neighborhood which, at that time, was the abode of wealth and culture. The building is one of a row, of a type to be seen in hundreds of other places, of brick and stone, four stories and a basement high, the upper floor being an attic. A heavy railing runs from in front of the basement up the broad front steps to the doorway. Inside, the rooms are large and comfortably arranged, and there was, in those days, quite a nice garden in the rear.

THEODORE ROOSEVELT'S BIRTHPLACE. 28 E. 20TH STREET, NEW YORK CITY.

THEODORE ROOSEVELT'S BIRTHPLACE. 28 E. 20TH STREET, NEW YORK CITY.

It can truthfully be said that Theodore Roosevelt comes from a race of soldiers and statesmen, and that Dutch, Scotch, French, and Irish blood flows in his veins. This being so, it is no wonder that, when the Spanish-American War broke out, he closed his desk as Assistant Secretary of the Navy, saying,

"My duty here is done; my place is in the field," and went forth to win glory on the battle-field of San Juan Hill.

Five generations of Roosevelts lived in or near New York previous to the birth of Theodore Roosevelt, the father of the President, in 1831. Nearly all were well-to-do, and many served the city and the state as aldermen and members of the legislature. During the Revolution they followed under Washington's banner, and their purses were wide open to further the cause of independence.

Theodore Roosevelt the elder was a merchant and banker; a man broad in his views and filled with the spirit of genuine philanthropy. He founded one of the hospitals of the city and was at one time chairman of the State Board of Charities. A story is told of him which is probably true. One day Charles Loring Brace came to him for financial assistance in establishing homes for the little waifs of the city.

"I will see what I can do," said Mr. Roosevelt. "But you know that just at present I am busy with other charitable works."

"I know that," said Mr. Brace. "But what I ask for is very much needed. The waifs and poor, homeless newsboys have no shelter."

The next day, when returning from the establishment in which he was a partner, Mr. Roosevelt came upon a newsboy sitting on a doorstep, crying bitterly.

"What is the matter, my little man?" he asked.

"I lost me money; it dropped down into de sewer hole!" sobbed the ragged urchin. "Every cent of it is gone."

Mr. Roosevelt questioned the lad and found out that the boy had no home and that his only relative was a longshoreman who was hardly ever sober. He gave the lad some money to replace the amount lost, and the next day sent word to Mr. Brace that he would do all he possibly could toward establishing the waifs' shelters that were so much needed. The Newsboys' Lodging House of New York City is one of the results of Mr. Roosevelt's practical charities. He also did much to give criminals a helping hand when they came from prison, stating that that was the one time in their lives when they most needed help, for fear they might slip back into their previous bad habits.

In 1853 Theodore Roosevelt the elder married Miss Martha Bullock, of Roswell, Cobb County, Georgia. Miss Bullock was the daughter of Major James S. Bullock and a direct descendant of Archibald Bullock, the first governor of Georgia. It will thus be seen that the future President had both Northern and Southern blood in his make-up, and it may be added here that during the terrible Civil War his relatives were to be found both in the Union and the Confederate ranks. Mrs. Roosevelt was a strong Southern sympathizer, and when a certain gathering, during the Civil War, was in progress at the Roosevelt city home, she insisted upon displaying a Confederate flag at one of the windows.

"I am afraid it will make trouble," said Mr. Roosevelt; and he was right. Soon a mob began to gather in the street, clamoring that the flag be taken down.

"I shall not take it down," said Mrs. Roosevelt, bravely. "The room is mine, and the flag is mine. I love it, and nobody shall touch it. Explain to the crowd that I am a Southern woman and that I love my country."

There being no help for it, Mr. Roosevelt went to the front door and explained matters as best he could. A few in the crowd grumbled, but when Mrs. Roosevelt came to the window and looked down on the gathering, one after another the men went away, and she and her flag remained unmolested.

Theodore Roosevelt, the future President, was one of a family of four. He had a brother Elliott and two sisters. His brother was several years younger than himself, but much more robust, and would probably have lived many years and have distinguished himself, had he not met death in a railroad accident while still a young man.

In the years when Theodore Roosevelt was a boy, New York City was not what it is to-day. The neighborhood in which he lived was, as I have already mentioned, a fashionable one, and the same may be said of many other spots near to Union Square, where tall business blocks were yet unknown. The boys and girls loved to play in the little park and on the avenue, and here it was that the rather delicate schoolboy grew to know Edith Carew, who lived in Fourteenth Street and who was his school companion. Little did they dream in those days, as they played together, that one day he would be President and she his loving wife, the mistress of the White House.

Mr. Roosevelt was a firm believer in public institutions, and he did not hesitate to send his children to the public schools, especially his boys, that they might come in direct personal contact with the great outside world. So to a near-by institution of learning Theodore and Elliott trudged day after day, with their school-books under their arms, just as thousands of other schoolboys are doing to-day. But in those days there were few experiments being tried in the schools, and manual training and the like were unknown. The boys were well grounded in reading, writing, and arithmetic, as well as spelling, history, and geography, and there was great excitement when a "spelling-bee" was in progress, to see who could spell the rest of the class or the gathering down.

It is said upon good authority that Theodore Roosevelt was a model scholar from the start. He loved to read Cooper's "Leatherstocking Tales," and works of travel, and preferred books above anything else. But when he found that constant studying was ruining his constitution, he determined to build himself up physically as well as mentally.

In the summer time the family often went to the old Roosevelt "out of town" mansion on Long Island. This was called "Tranquillity," a fine large place near Oyster Bay, set in a grove of beautiful trees. The journey to "Tranquillity" was in those days a tedious one, but the Roosevelt children did not mind it, and once at the old place they were certain of a good time so long as their vacation lasted. Here it was that Theodore Roosevelt learned to ride on horseback and how to handle a gun. And here, too, the boys would go boating, fishing, and bathing, to their hearts' content.

Mr. Theodore Roosevelt the elder was a member of the Dutch Reformed Church, and the religious teaching of his children was not neglected. At an early age the future President became a member of that denomination and has remained a member ever since. The church was on the East Side, and had high-backed pews, and here were delivered sermons that were as long as they were full of strength and wisdom. That these sermons had their full effect upon the future President is shown by his addresses delivered before the Young Men's Christian Association of New York City and a church community of the West, years later. In addressing the Young Men's Christian Association Mr. Roosevelt, who was then governor of the State, said:

"The vice of envy is not only dangerous, but also a mean vice, for it is always a confession of inferiority. It may provoke conduct which will be fruitful of wrong to others; and it must cause misery to the man who feels it. It will not be any the less fruitful of wrong and misery if, as is often the case with evil motives, it adopts some high-sounding alias. The truth is, gentlemen, that each one of us has in him certain passions and instincts which, if they gain the upper hand in his soul, would mean that the wild beast had come uppermost in him. Envy, malice, and hatred are such passions, and they are just as bad if directed against a class or group of men as if directed against an individual."

Golden words, well worth remembering. A person who believes in them with all his heart cannot go far wrong in his actions, no matter what his station in life.

CHAPTER II

NICKNAMED TEDDY GOES TO HARVARD COLLEGE MEMBER OF MANY CLUBS DEATH OF MR. ROOSEVELT ANECDOTES OF COLLEGE LIFE

The instincts of the hunter must have been born in Theodore Roosevelt. His first gun was given to him when he was ten years of age, and for the time being his books and his studies were forgotten, and he devoted his whole time and attention to shooting at a target set up in the garden of the country home and in going out with the older folks after such small game as were to be found in that vicinity.

The horses on the place were his pets, and he knew the peculiarities of each as well as did the man who cared for them. Riding and driving came to him as naturally as breathing, and the fact that a steed was mettlesome did not daunt him.

"My father often drove four-in-hand," he has said. "I liked very much to go with him, and I liked to drive, too."

Theodore Roosevelt's schoolboy days were not far out of the ordinary. He studied hard, and if he failed in a lesson he did his best to make it up the next time. It is well said that there is no royal road to learning, and even a future President must study just as hard as his classmates if he wants to keep up with them. Sometimes he was absent from school on account of sickness, and then it was a sharp struggle to keep from dropping behind.

"In those days nobody expected Teddy Roosevelt to amount to a great deal," some one has said. "He was thin, pale, and delicate, and suffered with his eyes. But he pulled through, and when he took to athletics, it was wonderful how he got stronger."

By his intimate companions, and indeed by nearly everybody who knew him, he was called Teddy, and this nickname clung to him when he went forth into the great world to become a governor and a president. How the nickname came first into use is not known.

Since those schoolboy days Mr. Roosevelt has been asked this question:

"What did you expect to be, or dream of being, when you were a boy?"

"I do not recollect that I dreamed at all or planned at all," was the answer. "I simply obeyed the injunction, 'Whatever thy hand findeth to do, do that with all thy might,' and so I took up what came along as it came."

In 1876, while the great Centennial Exhibition was being held at Philadelphia in commemoration of one hundred years of national liberty, Theodore Roosevelt took up his residence at Cambridge, Massachusetts, and became a student at Harvard College. During the previous year his health had been poor indeed, but now he had taken hold of himself in earnest.

"I determined to be strong and well, and did everything to make myself so," he has said. "By the time I entered Harvard I was able to take part in whatever sports I liked."

As perhaps some of my readers know, Harvard College (now termed a University) is the oldest and largest institution of learning in the United States. It was founded in 1636, and among its graduates numbered John Quincy Adams, sixth President of our country. The college proper is located in Cambridge, but some of the attached schools are in Boston.

Theodore Roosevelt was rich enough to have lived in elegant style while at Harvard, but he preferred unostentatious quarters, and took two rooms in the home of Benj. H. Richardson, at what was then No. 16 and is now No. 88 Winthrop Street. The residence is a neat and comfortable one, standing on the southwest corner of Winthrop and Holyoke streets.

The young student had two rooms on the second floor, one of good size, used for a study, and a small bedroom. In the whole four years he was at the college he occupied these rooms, and he spent a great deal of time in fixing them up to suit his own peculiar taste. On the walls were all sorts of pictures and photographs, along with foils and boxing-gloves, and the horns of wild animals. On a shelf rested some birds which he had himself stuffed, and books were everywhere.

HOUSE IN WHICH THEODORE ROOSEVELT ROOMED WHILE AT HARVARD.

"It was a regular den, and typical of Roosevelt to the last degree," a student of those times has said. "He had his gun there and his fishing rod, and often spoke of using them. He was noted for trying to get at the bottom of things, and I remember him well on one occasion when I found him with a stuffed bird in one hand and a natural history in the other, trying to decide if the description in the volume covered the specimen before him." When Roosevelt graduated from college, he was one of a very few that took honors, and the subject of his essay was natural history. How his love of natural history continued will be shown later when we see him as a ranchman and hunter of the West.

Theodore Roosevelt had decided to make the most of himself, and while at Harvard scarcely a moment was wasted. If he was not studying, he was in the gymnasium or on the field, doing what he could to make himself strong. He was a firm believer in the saying that a sound body makes a sound mind, and he speedily became a good boxer, wrestler, jumper, and runner. He wrestled a great deal, and of this sport says:

"I enjoyed it immensely and never injured myself. I think I was a good deal of a wrestler, and though I never won a championship, yet more than once I won my trial heats and got into the final rounds."

At running he was equally good. "I remember once we had a stiff run out into the country," said a fellow-student. "Roosevelt was behind at the start, but when all of the others got played out he forged ahead, and in the end he beat us by several minutes. But he never bragged about it. You see, it wasn't his style."

With all his other sports, and his studying, the young collegian did not give up his love for driving. He had a good horse and a fancy cart, one of the elevated sort with large wheels, and in this turnout he was seen many a day, driving wherever it pleased him to go. Sometimes he would get on the road with other students, and then there was bound to be more or less racing.

With a strong love for natural history it was not surprising that he joined the Natural History Club of the college, and of this he was one of the most active members. He also joined the Athletic Association, of which he was a steward, and the Art Club, the Rifle Corps, the O.K. Society, and the Finance Club. In his senior year he became a member of the Porcellian Club, the Hasty Pudding, and the Alpha Delta Phi Club, and also one of the editors of a college paper called the *Advocate*. On Sundays he taught a class of boys, first in a mission school, and then in a Congregational Sunday school. It was a life full of planning, full of study, and full of work, and it suited Theodore Roosevelt to the last degree.

As he grew older his love of natural history was supplemented by a love for the history of nations, and particularly by a love of the history of his own country. The war of 1812 interested him intensely, and before he graduated he laid plans for writing a history of this war, which should go into all the details of the memorable naval conflicts.

It was while in his third year at Harvard that Theodore Roosevelt suffered the first heavy affliction of his life. On February 9, 1878, his father died. It was a cruel blow to the family, and one from which the faithful wife scarcely recovered. The son at Harvard felt his loss greatly, and it was some time before he felt able to resume his studies. The elder Roosevelt's work as a philanthropist was well known, and many gathered at his bier to do him honor, while the public journals were filled with eulogies of the man. The poor mourned bitterly that he was gone, and even the newsboys were filled with regret over his taking away. In speaking of his parent, President Roosevelt once said: "I can remember seeing him going down Broadway, staid and respectable business man that he was, with a poor sick kitten in his coat pocket, which he had picked up in the street." Such a man could not but have a heart overflowing with goodness.

While at college Theodore Roosevelt often showed that self-reliance for which he has since become famous. To every study that he took up he applied himself closely, and if he was not at the head of the class, he was by no means near the foot. When he was sure of a thing, no amount of argument could convince him that he was wrong, and he did not hesitate at times to enter into a discussion even with some of the professors over him.

Although a close student, and also a good all-round athlete, Theodore Roosevelt did not forget his social opportunities. Boston was but a short distance from his rooms in Cambridge, and thither he often went to visit the people he had met or to whom he had letters of introduction. He was always welcome, for his manner was a winning one, and he usually had something to tell that was of interest something of what he had seen or done, of the next foot-ball or base-ball game, of the coming boat races, of his driving or exploring, or of how he had added a new stuffed bird to his collection, or a new lizard, and of how a far-away friend had sent him a big turtle as a souvenir of an ocean trip in the South Seas. There is a story that this big turtle got loose one night and alarmed the entire household by crawling through the hallway, looking for a pond or mud-hole in which to wallow. At first the turtle was mistaken for a burglar, but he soon revealed himself by his angry snapping, and it was hard work making him a prisoner once more.

CHAPTER III

MARRIES MISS ALICE LEE TRAVELS IN EUROPE BOLD MOUNTAIN-CLIMBING STUDYING LAW IN NEW YORK ELECTED TO THE ASSEMBLY PERSONAL ENCOUNTER WITH THE ENEMY

It was a proud and happy day for Theodore Roosevelt when, in the summer of 1880, he was graduated from Harvard. He took scholarly as well as social honors, and came forth a Phi Beta Kappa man. His fellow-students wished him well, and his family greeted him most affectionately.

Yet with it all there was just a bit of melancholy in this breaking away from a place that had been as a second home to him for four long years. The students were scattering to the four points of the compass, and he might never see some of them again. But others were there whom he was to meet later, and who were destined to march under him up the bullet-swept slopes of San Juan in far-away Cuba. But at that time there was no thought of war and carnage, only good-fellowship, with addresses and orations, music, flying flags, and huge bonfires and fireworks at night. Happy college days were they, never to be forgotten.

THEODORE ROOSEVELT AT GRADUATION, 1880.

THEODORE ROOSEVELT AT GRADUATION, 1880.

While a student at Harvard, Theodore Roosevelt had become intimately acquainted with Miss Alice Lee, of Boston, a beautiful girl who was a member of an aristocratic family of that city. The young college student was a frequent visitor at the home of the Lees, and on September 23, 1880, the two were married.

It had been decided that Theodore Roosevelt should travel in Europe after graduating. His father had left the family well provided for, so there was no rush to get into something whereby a living might be earned. Yet Theodore Roosevelt had long since determined not to be an idler. He would travel and improve his mind, and then settle down to that for which he seemed best fitted.

To Europe then he went, accompanied by his bride, to study a little and to visit the art galleries and museums, the palaces of kings and queens, and the many great cities of that continent. He travelled through Italy, Switzerland, Germany, France, and the British Isles, taking note of everything he saw and comparing it with what he had seen in his own country. When in lower Europe, the spirit of adventure seized him, and he climbed those lofty mountains of the Alps, the Jungfrau and the Matterhorn, and for those deeds of daring was made a member of the Alpine Club of London. It may be mentioned here that climbing the mountains mentioned is a very difficult feat, and that more than one traveller has lost his life in such attempts. The peaks are covered with snow and ice; the path from one cliff to the next is narrow and uncertain, and a fall into some dark and fearful hollow usually means death. But the danger only urged Theodore Roosevelt on, and added zest to the undertaking.

He was intensely interested in all he saw, both in Europe proper and in the British Isles, but wrote that he was glad to get back home again, among his own people. To him there was no country like America, the land of *Golden Opportunity*, as one of our most noted writers has called it. In Europe there was more or less a lack of personal liberty; here a man could try to make what he pleased of himself, be it cobbler or President.

The young college graduate had an uncle in New York, named Robert B. Roosevelt, who was a well-known lawyer. On his return to this country Theodore Roosevelt entered his uncle's office, and likewise took up the study of law at Columbia University, attending the lectures given by Professor Dwight. Here again his search after what he termed "bottom facts" came to light, and he is well remembered as a member of the law class because of the way he frequently asked questions and called for explanations accepting nothing as a fact until it was perfectly clear in his own mind. The interruptions did not always suit the professor or the other students, yet they were often the means of clearing up a point that was hazy to many others who had not the courage to thrust forth their inquiries as did Theodore Roosevelt.

"He wants to know it all," said one student, in disgust.

"Well, never mind; I wish I knew it all," answered another. "I guess he knows what he is doing." And in this he was right; Theodore Roosevelt knew exactly what he was trying to accomplish.

The young man was now twenty-three years of age, broad-shouldered, and in much better health than ever before. He had not abandoned his athletic training, and would often run out to the old home at Oyster Bay for a tramp into the woods or on a hunting tour.

While still studying law, Theodore Roosevelt entered politics by taking an active part in a Republican primary. He lived in the twenty-third assembly district of the state. The district included a great number of rich and influential citizens, and on that account was called the "Diamond Back District."

"Let us put up young Roosevelt for Assembly," said one of the politicians. "He's a clever fellow."

"That may be," said another. "But I don't know that we can manage him. He seems a fellow who wants his own way."

"Yes, he'll want his own way, but I reckon that way will be the right way," put in a third speaker.

No sooner had Theodore Roosevelt's name been mentioned as a possible candidate than there was a storm of opposition from some politicians who had in the past ruled the district with a rod of iron. It was a Republican district, so that the contest for the place was entirely in the primary.

"If he is nominated and elected, our power will be gone," they told themselves; and set to work without delay to throw the nomination into the hands of somebody else.

Theodore Roosevelt suspected what was going on, but he said nothing to those who opposed him. With his friends he was very frank, and told them that if he was nominated he would do his best to win the election and serve them honestly in the legislature.

His open-heartedness won him many friends, and when the primary was held, those who had opposed him were chagrined to see him win the nomination with votes to spare. Some at once predicted that he would not be elected.

"Those who opposed him at the primary will not vote for him," they said. "They would rather help the Democrats."

But this prediction proved false. At the election Theodore Roosevelt was elected with a good majority. It was his first battle in the political arena and if he felt proud over it, who can blame him?

The State Capitol of New York is, as my young readers must know, at Albany, on the Upper Hudson, and hither the young assemblyman journeyed. The assemblymen poured in from all over the state, and were made up of all sorts and conditions of men, including bankers, farmers, merchants, contractors, liquor dealers, and even prize-fighters. Many of these men were thoroughly honest, but there were others who were there for gain only, and who cared little for the passing of just laws.

The party to which Theodore Roosevelt belonged was in the minority, so that the young assemblyman found he would have to struggle hard if he expected to be heard at all. But the thoughts of such a struggle only put him on his mettle, and he plunged in with a vigor that astonished his opponents and caused great delight to his friends.

"He is fearless," said one who had voted for him. "He will make things warm for those who don't want to act on the square." And he certainly did make it warm, until a certain class grew to fear and hate him to such a degree that they plotted to do him bodily harm.

"He has got to learn that he must mind his own business," was the way one of these corruptionists reasoned.

"But what can we do?" asked another. "He's as sharp on the floor of the Assembly as a steel trap."

"We'll get Stubby to brush up against him," said a third.

Stubby was a bar-room loafer who had been at one time something of a pugilist. He was a thoroughly unprincipled fellow, and it was known that he would do almost anything for money.

"Sure, I'll fix him," said Stubby. "You just leave him to me and see how I polish him off."

The corruptionists and their tool met at the Delavan House, an old-fashioned hotel at which politicians in and around the capital were wont to congregate, and waited for the young assemblyman. Roosevelt was not long in putting in an appearance and was soon in deep discussion with some friends.

"Watch him, Stubby," said one of the young assemblyman's enemies. "Don't let him get away from you to-night."

"I have me eye on him," answered Stubby.

Roosevelt was on the way to the buffet of the hotel when the crowd, with Stubby in front, pushed against him rudely. The young assemblyman stepped back and viewed those before him fearlessly.

"Say, what do yer mean, running into me that way?" demanded Stubby, insolently.

As he spoke he aimed a savage blow at Theodore Roosevelt. But the young assemblyman had not forgotten how to box, and he dodged with an agility that was astonishing.

"This fellow needs to be taught a lesson," Theodore Roosevelt told himself, and then and there he proceeded to administer the lesson in a manner that Stubby never forgot. He went down flat on his back, and when he got up, he went down again, with a bleeding nose and one eye all but closed. Seeing this, several leaped in to his assistance, but it was an ill-fated move, for Roosevelt turned on them also, and down they went, too; and then the encounter came to an end, with Theodore Roosevelt the victor.

"And that wasn't the end of it," said one, who witnessed the affair. "After it was over young Roosevelt was as smiling as ever. He walked straight over to some of his enemies who had been watching the mix-up from a distance and told them very plainly that he knew how the attack had originated, and he was much obliged to them, for he hadn't enjoyed himself so much for a year. Phew! but weren't those fellows mad! And wasn't Stubby mad when he learned that they had set him against one of the best boxers Harvard ever turned out? But after that you can make sure they treated Roosevelt with respect and gave him a wide berth."

CHAPTER IV

THEODORE ROOSEVELT AND GOVERNOR CLEVELAND GOOD WORK AS AN ASSEMBLYMAN SOME MEASURES PUSHED THROUGH BIRTH OF ALICE ROOSEVELT DEATH OF MR. ROOSEVELT'S MOTHER

The career of an assemblyman is not generally an interesting one, but Mr. Roosevelt managed to extract not a little pleasure and also some profit from it. The experience was just what he needed to fit himself for the larger positions he was, later on, to occupy.

One happening is of peculiar interest to note. While Theodore Roosevelt was a member of the Assembly, Grover Cleveland became governor of the state. Mr. Cleveland was a Democrat, while Mr. Roosevelt was a Republican, yet the two future Presidents of the United States became warm friends, a friendship that has endured to the present day.

It is said that the friendship started in rather a peculiar manner. There was at the time a measure before the Assembly to reduce the fare of the elevated roads in New York City from ten cents to five cents. After a great deal of talking, the bill passed the Assembly and then the Senate, and went to the governor for his signature. Much to the surprise of the general public Governor Cleveland vetoed the bill, stating that when the capitalists had built the elevated roads they had understood that the fare was to be ten cents, and that it was not right to deprive them of their profits. At once those who wanted the measure to become a law decided to pass it over the governor's head. When this attempt was made, Theodore Roosevelt got up boldly and said he could not again vote for the bill that he was satisfied that Governor Cleveland's view of the matter was correct.

"These people would not have put their money in the elevated railroads had they not been assured that the fare was to be ten cents," said he. "We are under obligation to them, and we must keep our promises." And so the bill fell through. It was not in itself right that the fare should be ten cents, and it has long since been reduced to five cents, but it shows that Theodore Roosevelt was bound to do what was right and just, according to the dictates of his own conscience, and this won for him many friends, even among those who had opposed him politically.

In a work of this kind, intended mainly for the use of young people, it is not necessary to do more than glance at the work which Theodore Roosevelt accomplished while a member of the New York Assembly.

He made a close study of the various political offices of New York County and discovered that many office-holders were drawing large sums of money in the shape of fees for which they were doing hardly any work. This he considered unfair, and by dint of hard labor helped to pass a law placing such offices on the salary list, making a saving to the county of probably half a million dollars a year.

One of the best things done by Theodore Roosevelt at that time was the support given by him to a civil service law for the state. Up to that time office-holding was largely in the hands of the party which happened to be in power.

"This is all wrong," said the young assemblyman. "A clerk or anybody else doing his duty faithfully should not be thrown out as soon as there is a political change." The new law was passed, and this was the beginning of what is commonly called the merit system, whereby a large number of those who work for the state are judged solely by their capabilities and not by their political beliefs. This system has since been extended to other states and also to office-holding under the national government.

Another important measure pushed through the Assembly by Theodore Roosevelt was what was known as the Edson Charter for New York City, giving to the mayor certain rights which in the past had rested in the board of aldermen. This measure was defeated during Roosevelt's second term of office, but in 1884 he pressed it with such force that it overcame all opposition and became a law. Many have considered this victory his very best work.

By those who knew him at this time he is described as having almost a boyish figure, frank face, clear, penetrating eyes, and a smile of good-natured friendship and dry humor. When he talked it was with an earnestness that could not be mistaken. By those who were especially bitter against him he was sometimes called a dude and a silk stocking, but to these insinuations he paid no attention, and after the encounter at the Delavan House his opponents were decidedly more careful as to how they addressed him.

"Take him all the way through he was generally even tempered," one has said who met him at that time. "But occasionally there was a flash from his eye that made his opponent draw back in quick order. He would stand a good deal, but there were some things he wouldn't take, and they knew it. One thing is certain, after he was in the Assembly for a few months everybody knew perfectly that to come to him with any bill that was the least bit shady was a waste of time and effort. Roosevelt wouldn't stand for it a minute."

In those days Theodore Roosevelt did not give up his habits of athletic exercise, and nearly every day he could be seen taking long walks in the country around Albany. In the meantime his "Naval War of 1812" was well under way, but he could spare only a few hours occasionally to complete his manuscript.

His married life had thus far been a happy one, and its joy was greatly increased by the birth of his daughter Alice. As will be seen later, Mr. Roosevelt is what is called a family man, and he took great comfort in this new addition to his little household. But his happiness was short-lived, for in 1884, when the daughter was but a baby, the beloved wife died, and the little one had to be given over to the care of the grandparents in Boston. Not many months later Mr. Roosevelt's mother died also, heaping additional sorrow upon his head.

With the conclusion of his third term in the Assembly Theodore Roosevelt's work as a member of that body came to an end. If he had made some enemies, he had made more friends, and he was known as an ardent supporter of reform in all branches of politics. In recognition of his ability he was chosen as a delegate-at-large to the Republican convention brought together to nominate a candidate to succeed President Arthur.

At that time James G. Blaine from Maine had served many years in the United States Senate, and it was thought that he would surely be both nominated and elected. But many were opposed to Blaine, thinking he would not support such reform measures as they wished to see advanced, and among this number was Theodore Roosevelt.

"We must nominate Mr. Edmunds," said the young delegate-at-large, and did his best for the gentleman in question.

"It cannot be done," said another delegate.

The convention met at Exposition Hall in Chicago, and Mr. Roosevelt was placed on the Committee on Resolutions. It was a stormy convention, and ballot after ballot had to be taken before a nomination could be secured. Blaine led from the start, with Senator Edmunds a fairly close second.

"If Blaine is nominated, he will be defeated," said more than one.

At last came the deciding vote, and James G. Blaine was put up at the head of the ticket, with John A. Logan for Vice-President.

At once Blaine clubs were organized all over the country, and the Republican party did all in its power to elect its candidate. He was called the Plumed Knight, and many political clubs wore plumes in his honor when on parade. In the meantime the Democrats had nominated Grover Cleveland.

The fight was exceedingly bitter up to the very evening of election day. When the votes were counted, it was found that Blaine had been defeated by a large majority, and that Grover Cleveland, Roosevelt's old friend, had won the highest gift in the hands of the nation.

His work at the convention in Chicago was Theodore Roosevelt's first entrance into national affairs, and his speeches on that occasion will not be readily forgotten. It was here that he came into contact with William McKinley, with whom, sixteen years later, he was to run on the same ticket. The records of that convention show that on one occasion McKinley spoke directly after Roosevelt. Thus were these two drawn together at that early day without knowing or dreaming that one was to succeed the other to the Presidency.

But though Theodore Roosevelt was disappointed over the nomination made at Chicago, he did not desert his party. Instead he did all he could to lead them to victory, until the death of his mother caused him to withdraw temporarily from public affairs.

Alice Lee Roosevelt

CHAPTER V

THEODORE ROOSEVELT AS A RANCHMAN AND HUNTER IN THE BAD LANDS BRINGING DOWN HIS FIRST BUFFALO RATTLESNAKES, AND A WILD GOOSE

Theodore Roosevelt had now published his "Naval History of the War of 1812," and it had created a decidedly favorable opinion among those critics who were best able to judge of the production. It is an authoritative work, and is to-day in the library of nearly every American war-ship afloat, as well as in numerous government libraries in this country, as at Washington, West Point, and Annapolis, and also in leading libraries of England.

Being out of politics the young author thought of taking up his pen once more. But he was restless by nature, and the loss of his wife and his mother still weighed heavily upon him. So he took himself to the West, to where the Little Missouri River flows in winding form through what are called the Bad Lands of North Dakota.

Here, on the edge of the cattle country, Theodore Roosevelt had become possessed of two ranches, one called the Elkhorn and the other Chimney Butte. Both were located by the river, which during the dry season was hardly of any depth at all, but which during the heavy rains, or during the spring freshets, became a roaring torrent.

At one of these ranches Theodore Roosevelt settled down for the time being, to rough it in hunting and raising cattle. When the weather would not permit of his going abroad, or when the mood of the author seized him, he wrote. As a result of these experiences he has given us a delightful work called "The Hunting Trips of a Ranchman," first published in 1885, giving his adventures among the cattle and while on the hunt, sometimes alone and sometimes in company with the rude but honest cow punchers and plainsmen who surrounded him.

Mr. Roosevelt has described the ranch at which he lived for the greater part of his time as a long, low, story-high house of hewn logs, clean and neat, and with many rooms. It faced the river, and in front was a long, low veranda, where one might idle on a clear, warm day to his heart's content. Inside, the main room contained a shelf full of the owner's favorite outdoor books and the walls half-a-dozen pet pictures. Rifles and shot-guns stood handy in corners, and on pegs and deer horns hung overcoats of wolf or coon skin and gloves of otter or beaver.

That Theodore Roosevelt was a close observer of all that occurred around him is proved by his writings. With great minuteness he has described his life at the ranch home and while in the saddle, both in winter and summer, telling of his experiences while rounding up cattle and while bringing down waterfowl and larger game of various kinds. He likewise describes the trained hunters he has met at different seasons of the year, and tells of what they have done or were trying to do.

At this time his favorite horse was a steed called Manitou. But when on a round-up of cattle, many ponies were taken along, so that a fresh mount could be had at any time. It was a breezy, free life, and to it our President undoubtedly owes the rugged constitution that he possesses to-day.

His observations led him to make many investigations concerning the smaller wild animals near his ranches and the larger beasts to be found farther off. The tales which were told to him by other ranchmen and hunters he always took "with a grain of salt," and he soon reached the conclusion that many of the so-styled mighty hunters were only such in name, and had brought down quantities of game only in years gone by when such game was plentiful and could be laid low without much trouble. Once when a man told him he had brought down a certain beast at four hundred yards, Roosevelt measured the distance and found it to be less than half that.

"You couldn't fool him on much," said one of the persons who met him about that time. "He would take precious little for granted. He wanted to know the how of everything, and he wasn't satisfied until he did know."

Regarding his own powers as a hunter at that time, Mr. Roosevelt is very modest. He says his eyesight was rather poor, and his hand not over steady, so that "drawing a bead" on anything was not easy. Yet he went into the sport with much enthusiasm, and if at times he came back at nightfall empty-handed, he did not complain, and he was almost certain to have something interesting to tell of what he had seen.

Theodore Roosevelt had been in this territory before, although not to remain any great length of time. Once he had come out to hunt buffalo, no easy thing to do, since this game was growing scarcer every day. He had a guide named Ferris, who was not particularly struck with the appearance of the pale young man, plainly dressed, whom he met at the railroad station.

"I sized him up as not being able to endure a long trip after a buffalo," said the guide, in speaking afterward of the meeting. "He was well mounted, but he looked as if he might play out before the sun went down."

But in this the guide was mistaken. Roosevelt proved that he could ride as well as anybody. The first night out found the hunters about thirty miles from any settlement. They went into camp on the open prairie, tethering their horses with ropes fastened to their saddles, which they used as pillows.

All went well for an hour or two, when the improvised pillow was jerked from beneath Theodore Roosevelt's head, and he heard his horse bounding away in the distance.

"Wolves!" cried the guide. "They have frightened our horses!"

So it proved; and the hunters lost no time in reaching for their firearms. But the wolves kept their distance, and soon Theodore Roosevelt was running after the horses, which, after a good deal of trouble, he secured and brought back. After that the guide no longer looked on him as a "tenderfoot."

"A tenderfoot," said he, "would have been scared to death. But Teddy Roosevelt was as cool as a cucumber through it all as if the happening wasn't in the least out of the ordinary."

For several days the hunters remained on the prairie looking for buffalo, but without success. They were on the point of turning back when the guide noticed that the horses were growing uneasy.

"Some big game at hand," he announced. "Come on to yonder washout and see if I am not right."

With great caution the hunters advanced to the washout the guide had mentioned. Dismounting, they crept forward in the shelter of the brushwood, and there, true enough, resting at his ease was a great buffalo bull.

"Hit him where the patch of red shows on his side," whispered the guide, and Roosevelt nodded to show that he understood. With care and coolness he took aim and fired, and the buffalo bull leaped up and staggered forward with the blood streaming from his mouth and nose.

"Shall I give him another?" was the question asked, but before it could be answered the buffalo bull gave a plunge and fell dead.

Rattlesnakes are rather unpleasant reptiles to deal with, and Theodore Roosevelt has shown his bravery by the way in which he speaks of them in his accounts of outdoor life. He says to a man wearing alligator boots there is little danger, for the fang of the reptile cannot go through the leather, and the snake rarely strikes as high as one's knee. But he had at least one experience with a rattlesnake not readily forgotten.

He was out on a hunt for antelope. The sage-brush in which he was concealing himself was so low that he had to crawl along flat on his breast, pushing himself forward with hands and feet as best he could.

He was almost on the antelope when he heard a warning whirr close at his side, and glancing hastily in that direction, saw the reptile but a few feet away, coiled up and ready to attack.

It was a thrilling and critical moment, and had the young hunter leaped up he might have been dangerously if not fatally struck. But by instinct he backed away silently and moved off in another direction through the brush. The rattlesnake did not follow, although it kept its piercing eyes on the hunter as long as possible. After the antelope stalk was over, Roosevelt came back to the spot, made a careful search, and, watching his chance, fired on the rattlesnake, killing it instantly.

In those days Theodore Roosevelt met Colonel William Cody, commonly known as "Buffalo Bill," and many other celebrated characters of the West. He never grew tired of listening to the stories these old trappers, hunters, scouts, and plainsmen had to tell, and some of these stories he afterward put into print, and they have made excellent reading.

During many of his hunting expeditions at that time Theodore Roosevelt was accompanied by his foreman, a good shot and all-round ranchman named Merrifield. Merrifield had been in the West but five years, but the life fitted him exactly, and in him Roosevelt the ranchman and hunter found a companion exactly to his liking, fearless and self-reliant to the last degree.

As perhaps most of my young readers know, wild geese are generally brought down with a shot-gun, but in the Bad Lands it was not unusual to bring them down with a rifle, provided the hunter was quick and accurate enough in his aim. One morning, just before dawn, Theodore Roosevelt was riding along the edge of a creek when he heard a cackling that he knew must come from some geese, and he determined if possible to lay one low.

It was easy work to dismount and crawl to the edge of the creek. But a fog lay over the water, and he could see the geese but indistinctly. Leaving the creek bank, he ran silently to where the watercourse made a turn and then crawled forward in the brush. Soon the fog lifted once more, and he saw the geese resting on the water close to the bend. He fired quickly and brought down the largest of the flock, while the others lost no time in disappearing. It was a good fat goose and made excellent eating.

CHAPTER VI

GROUSE AND OTHER SMALL GAME THE SCOTCHMAN AND THE SKUNK CAUGHT IN A HAILSTORM ON THE PRAIRIE BRINGING DOWN BLACK-TAIL DEER

It cannot be said that Theodore Roosevelt's venture as a ranchman was a very successful one, and it is doubtful if he expected to make much money out of it. He lost nothing in a financial way, and there is no doubt but that the experience was of great benefit to him. In this semi-wilderness he met all sorts and conditions of men, and grew to know them thoroughly. In the past his dealings had been almost entirely with people of large cities and towns, and with men of learning and large business affairs; here he fell in with the wildest kind of cowboys and frontiersmen. Some he soon found were not fit to be associated with, but the majority proved as honest and hard-working fellows as could be met with anywhere. Many of these loved the young "boss" from the start, and when, years later, the war with Spain broke out, and there was a call to arms, not a few of them insisted upon joining the Rough Riders just to be near Theodore Roosevelt once more.

Around the ranches owned by Theodore Roosevelt there were more or less grouse of the sharp-tailed variety. As this sort of game made excellent eating, ranchmen and regular hunters did not hesitate to bring them down at every opportunity.

One afternoon Theodore Roosevelt left his ranch to visit the shack of one of his herders, about thirty-five miles down the river. It was a cold, clear day, and he was finely mounted on a well-trained pony. He writes that he was after grouse, hoping to get quite a number of them.

He had trusted to reach the shack long before sundown, but the way was bad, over bottoms covered with thin ice and snow, and soon darkness came on, leaving him practically lost in the cottonwoods that lined the watercourse.

What to do the young ranchman did not know, and it is safe to say that he wished himself heartily out of the difficulty. It was so dark he could not see three yards ahead of him, and it was only by the merest accident that he struck the shack at last, and then he found it empty, for the herder had gone off elsewhere on business.

So far Roosevelt had seen no game, so he was without food, and what made matters worse, the larder of the shack proved to be empty. All he had with him was a little package of tea.

It was a dismal outlook truly, and especially on such a cold night. But firewood was at hand, and after turning his pony loose to shift for itself, the future President of our country started up housekeeping for himself by lighting a fire, bringing in some water from under the ice of the river, and brewing himself a good, strong cup of tea! It was not a very nourishing meal, but it was all he had, and soon after that he went to sleep, trusting for better luck in the morning.

He was up almost before daybreak, and my young readers can rest assured that by that time his appetite was decidedly keen. Listening intently, he could hear the grouse drumming in the woods close by.

"I must have some of them, and that directly," he told himself, and rifle in hand lost no time in making his way to the woods. By keeping out of sight behind the brushwood he managed to get quite close to the game, and so brought down one after another until he had five. Such success was a great satisfaction to him, and returning to the shack he fixed himself a breakfast of broiled sharptails, to which he did full justice.

It was not all play at the ranches, and sometimes Theodore Roosevelt went out with his men to round up the cattle and help "cut out" what was his own. This was hard work, for frequently the cattle did not want to be separated from the beasts belonging to another ranchman. More than once an angry cow or a bull would charge, and then there would be a lively scramble on pony-back or on foot to get out of the way. Sometimes, too, the cattle would wander off and get lost, and then a long and hard hunt would be necessary in order to find them again.

But there was fun as well as hard work, and Mr. Roosevelt has told one story about a skunk that is sure to be remembered. He says that skunks were very numerous, and that they were more feared than larger animals by the cowboys because the bite was sure to bring on hydrophobia.

One night a number of the cowboys and Mr. Roosevelt were sleeping in a hut. A skunk came along, and after a time worked its way into the hut. It got among the pots and pans and made a noise which quickly awoke a Scotchman named Sandy.

Thinking something was wrong, Sandy struck a light, and seeing the eyes of the skunk, fired. But his aim was bad, and the animal fled.

"What were you firing at?" asked half a dozen of the other cowboys.

The Scotchman explained, and, satisfied that it had been a skunk, the others told him he had better leave the animal alone or there would be trouble.

Nobody thought the skunk would come back, but it did, and again Sandy heard it among the pots and pans. This was too much for his Scotch blood, and taking aim once more, he fired and gave the skunk a mortal wound. At once the hut was filled with a powerful odor that made all the inmates rush for the open air.

"Now see what you have done!" cried several, indignantly.

"Hoot mon!" answered the Scotchman, holding his nose tightly, "A didna ken 'twould cause sec' a tragedee!"

And after that we may be sure that Sandy let skunks severely alone.

Hunting in the summer time, or when the weather was but moderately cold, was well enough, but hunting in the dead of winter was quite a different thing. Then the thermometer would frequently drop to thirty and forty degrees below zero, and there would be a cutting "norther" fit to freeze the very marrow in one's bones. Seldom was there much snow, but when it came, it caused a veritable blizzard, during which neither man nor beast felt like stirring out.

It was during such weather that Theodore Roosevelt once had the tip of his nose and one cheek frozen something that caused him not a little pain and trouble for a long time afterward.

It was in those dreary days that the logs were piled high in the broad fireplace of the ranch home, and Theodore Roosevelt spent his days in reading and studying, in writing letters to his friends and relatives, and in penning some of the hunting sketches that have won him literary fame.

One day, early in the winter, Theodore Roosevelt and his foreman went out to see if they could not bring in two white-tail deer which had been seen in the vicinity of the ranch the day before. One of the deer, a large buck, had been shot in the ankle by the foreman, so the beginning of the trail was easy to follow. The buck and his mate had gone into a thicket, and it was likely that there the pair had spent the night.

"We'll have our own trouble finding the tracks again," said the foreman. And so it proved; for during the night some cattle and other animals had passed in and out of the thicket, which covered a large extent of territory.

At last the hunters hit upon the right trail, and the foreman went ahead, leaving Roosevelt to keep somewhat toward the outside of the cover. Both were wide-awake and on the alert, and presently the foreman announced that he had found the spot where the wounded buck had passed the night.

"He is not very far from here," said the foreman, and hardly had he said this than Theodore Roosevelt heard a cracking of fallen twigs and a breaking of the brush and lower limbs of the trees as the buck rushed through the thicket. He ran with all speed in the direction and took station behind a large tree.

Only a few seconds passed, and then the buck showed his head and antlers among the brushwood. He was gazing ahead anxiously, no doubt trying to decide if it would be safe to leap into the open and run up the trail. Then he turned his gaze directly toward where Theodore Roosevelt was crouching, rifle in hand.

Another instant and it would have been too late. But just as the buck's head was turned and he sniffed the air suspiciously, the young ranchman pulled the trigger.

"He turned his head sharply toward me as I raised the rifle," says Mr. Roosevelt, in writing of this adventure, "and the bullet went fairly into his throat, just under the jaw, breaking his neck, and bringing him down in his tracks with hardly a kick."

The buck proved to be an extra fine one, and the two hunters lost no time in dressing the game and taking it to the ranch. Not wishing to go back for their horses, the two dragged the game over the snow, each taking hold of an antler for that purpose. It was intensely cold, so that each of the hunters had to drag first with one hand and then with the other for fear of having his fingers frozen.

This was one of the times when the young ranchman and hunter was successful in his quest. But Mr. Roosevelt has not hesitated to tell of the many times he has gone out on the hunt only to return empty-handed and glad enough to get back to a warm shelter and where he was sure of a good meal.

"Ranching and hunting was no bed of roses," some one who knew him at that time has said. "Many a time he came back utterly fagged out and not a thing to show for his labor. But he never complained, and on the contrary could generally tell a pretty good story about something he had seen or had taken note of. In the summer he would examine the nests of birds and waterfowl with great care, and I have seen him with a horned frog before him, studying every point of the creature."

Once while on the prairie the young ranchman was caught in a heavy hailstorm. He was out with a number of others, when, with scarcely any warning, the sky began to grow dark, and the wind came up in fitful gusts.

"We must get out of this, and quick too," said a companion. And all pushed onward as fast as they could. But soon the heavy fall of hail overtook them, and they were glad enough to seek even the slight shelter of a deep washout, where men and horses huddled close together for protection. The hailstones came down as large as marbles, causing the horses to jump around in a fashion that was particularly dangerous to themselves and to their owners. The time was August, yet the air grew very cold, and when the storm was over, some cattle were found completely benumbed. A few had been killed, and there had likewise been great slaughter among a flock of lambs that had been driven into the Bad Lands the year previous.

Mr. Roosevelt tells us that the greatest number of black-tailed deer he ever killed in one day was three. He is a true sportsman in this respect and does not kill for the mere sake of killing. Those who go out just to slaughter all they possibly can are not sportsmen, but butchers. To be sure, a hunter may have to play the butcher at times, when the meat is needed, but not otherwise.

On the occasion when the three black-tails were laid low the young ranchman and his foreman started on the hunt very early in the morning, when the bright moon was still in the sky. It was late in November and stinging cold, so they allowed their horses to take their own pace, which was far from slow.

The course of the hunters was up the bed of a dry creek, along which they passed the still sleeping cattle and also a drove of ponies. Then they reached a spot where they left their own steeds, and, rifles in hand, hurried silently toward a great plateau which lay some distance before them. Signs of deer could be seen on every hand, and both were certain that the day's outing would prove a grand success.

Theodore Roosevelt had separated from his companion when of a sudden he caught sight of a beautiful doe. It was a fair shot, and dropping on one knee he took aim and fired. But to his intense chagrin the doe bounded off and disappeared in the brushwood.

"Hit anything?" sang out the foreman.

"I am afraid not," was the answer.

"Never mind; better luck next time." And then both sank down behind a rock where they could get a good view of a hollow ahead of them.

They had been behind the rock but a short time when they heard a cracking of twigs, and a fine black-tail buck came cautiously into view. Both fired, and the buck rolled over, never to rise again. Then another deer came into view and both fired again, but the game was not struck and lost no time in disappearing.

"Never mind; one isn't so bad," said Theodore Roosevelt, and his companion agreed with him.

The hunters now decided to go forward into the hollow and look for the doe Theodore Roosevelt had missed. This was done, and soon the foreman pointed to some drops and splashes of blood.

"Must have hit her, after all," said the foreman. "We can take our time about following her up. We'll be sure to get her sooner or later."

But locating the wounded doe proved not so easy, after all. The trail was followed for some time, but was lost on the hard ground higher up; and at last the two hunters agreed to look for new game. They had lunch, and then started out nearly as fresh as before when suddenly the foreman called out:

"There's your game all right!"

He pointed to a clump of bushes, and running forward, both saw the doe stretched out, stiff and cold. She had been mortally wounded, after all, much to both hunters' gratification.

So far the hunting had been on foot, but now the hunters took again to their steeds. Mr. Roosevelt says he was wishing for just one more shot, to see if he could not do better than before, when his wish was gratified. Just ahead a yearling black-tail buck leaped into view and cantered away. After the buck went both hunters, but Theodore Roosevelt was in the lead, and this time determined to make no miss or poor shot. He waited until the buck turned its side to him, then fired with especial care. The game staggered on, then fell. The bullet had gone clean through its body, and in a few seconds it breathed its last.

CHAPTER VII

RUNS FOR MAYOR OF NEW YORK CITY MARRIAGE TO EDITH KERMIT CAREW HUNTING IN THE BIGHORN MOUNTAINS A WILD CHASE AFTER THREE ELK

Although Theodore Roosevelt was devoting himself to ranching, hunting, and literary work in North Dakota he had by no means given up his residence in New York or at Oyster Bay. More than this, he still continued his connection with the Republican party in spite of the set-back at the last National Convention.

In 1886, while Grover Cleveland was still President of the United States, there was an exceedingly sharp and bitter fight in New York City over the office of mayor. There was great discontent both in the Republican and the Democratic party, and nobody could tell what was going to happen on election day.

"Let us put up Teddy Roosevelt," said some of the Republicans, and shortly after this Theodore Roosevelt was nominated for mayor of New York. His regular opponent was Abram Hewitt, while the Independents put up Henry George, the "single tax" man, well known as the author of a book entitled "Progress and Poverty."

From the very start the campaign was an exceedingly hot one, and there was a good deal of parading and speech-making. Many clubs were organized in behalf of Theodore Roosevelt, and clubs were likewise formed to support the other candidates. The supporters of Henry George came from both regular parties, so political matters became very much mixed up.

"There is no show for Roosevelt unless George withdraws," said more than one old politician.

"And George won't withdraw," added others. And so it proved. Henry George was exceptionally strong with the poorer classes, and on election day he polled over 68,000 votes; 90,552 votes were cast for Hewitt, while Roosevelt received 60,435 votes.

It was certainly a disheartening defeat, and many a man would have retired from the political field, never to show himself again. But Theodore Roosevelt was made of sterner stuff. He held his ground and went his way as before, resolved to do his duty as it should present itself.

It was about this time that his intimacy with Miss Edith Kermit Carew was renewed. It will be remembered that she had been his playmate during his earlier days around Union Square. In the years that had followed she had been graduated from a young ladies' seminary and had travelled abroad, visiting London, Paris, and other large cities. Now she was home again, and on December 2, 1886, she became Mr. Roosevelt's wife.

Mr. Roosevelt's second marriage has been a very happy one. Mrs. Roosevelt is a loving wife and a gracious mistress of the White House. Five children have come to bless their union, of which more will be said later. Mrs. Roosevelt at once took Mr. Roosevelt's daughter Alice to her heart, and from that time to this the two have been as mother and daughter.

Theodore Roosevelt had already produced his "Naval War of 1812" and his "Hunting Trips of a Ranchman," both spoken of in previous pages. A short while after he was married the second time he brought out a "Life of Thomas Benton," and a year later a "Life of Gouverneur Morris." In addition to this he wrote a number of articles for the magazines, and also some short stories for young folks. All were well received and added not a little to his literary reputation.

But the desire to be out in the open, to roam the prairie and to hunt, was in his veins, and again and again he visited his ranches in the Bad Lands, and took hunting trips in other directions. Sometimes he cared little or nothing for the game brought down, and at others he went on the hunt with great deliberation, for "something worth while," as he expressed it.

How careful he could be on the latter occasions is shown by his printed views on hunting, in which he discusses the best rifles, shot-guns, and pistols to use, the best knives to carry, how to dress with comfort, and how to follow up game, on horseback and on foot, in the open and when in the woods or in the short brush. He has also told us much about the habits of the beasts and birds that he has hunted, showing that he followed the sport intelligently and not in the haphazard fashion of many who go out merely to get a big bagful of game.

Edith Kermit Roosevelt

Hunting was not all fun in those days. We have already related how Theodore Roosevelt was caught in a heavy hailstorm. At another time he and his companions were caught in a three-days' rain-storm, during which the wind blew a hurricane. They were miles away from the ranch home, and it was utterly impossible to move in any direction.

"Reckon we are booked to stay here," said one of the cowboys, a fellow from the South. "It's a right smart storm, and it's going to stay by us." And stay by them it did, until the party were almost out of provisions. They got what shelter they could in something of a hollow overhung with trees and brush, but this was not very satisfactory, and all were soaked to the skin, and the blankets in which they rolled themselves at night were both wet and muddy.

"Teddy Roosevelt didn't like that wetting, and I know it," one of the cowboys has said since. "But he didn't grumble near as much as some of the others. We had to take our medicine, and he took his like a man."

There were no elk in the immediate vicinity of Theodore Roosevelt's ranches, nor were there many bears or buffaloes. But all of these animals were to be met with further westward, and the young ranchman had been after them during a previous year's hunting while on a trip to Montana and Wyoming.

At that time the destination of the party was the Bighorn Mountains, which were reached only after a painful and disheartening journey over a very uncertain Indian trail, during which one of the ponies fell into a washout and broke his neck, and a mule stuck fast in a mud-hole and was extricated only after hours of hard work.

"It was on the second day of our journey into the mountains that I got my first sight of elk," says Mr. Roosevelt. The party was on the trail leading into a broad valley, moving slowly and cautiously along through a patch of pine trees. When the bottom of the valley was gained, Mr. Roosevelt saw a herd of cow elk at a great distance, and soon after took a shot at one, but failed to reach his mark.

"I'm going after that herd," he said. And as soon as the party had pitched camp, he sallied forth in one direction, while his foreman, Merrifield, took another.

As Theodore Roosevelt had supposed, the elk had gone off in a bunch, and for some distance it was easy to follow them. But further on the herd had spread out, and he had to follow with more care, for fear of getting on the wrong trail, for elk tracks ran in all directions over the mountains. These tracks are there to-day, but the elk and the bears are fast disappearing, for ruthless hunters have done their best to exterminate the game.

After passing along for several miles, Theodore Roosevelt felt he must be drawing close to the herd. Just then his rifle happened to tap on the trunk of a tree, and instantly he heard the elk moving away in new alarm. His hunting blood was now aroused, and he rushed forward with all speed, but as silently as possible. By taking a short cut, the young ranchman managed to come up beside the running elk. They were less than twenty yards away, and had it not been for the many trees which were on every side, he would have had an excellent shot at them. As it was he brought low a fine, full-grown cow elk, and hit a bull calf in the hind leg. Later on he took up the trail of the calf and finished that also.

Of this herd the foreman also brought down two, so that for the time being the hunters had all the meat they needed. But Theodore Roosevelt was anxious to obtain some elk horns as trophies of the chase, and day after day a watch was kept for bull elk, as the hunters moved the camp from one place to another.

At last the long-looked-for opportunity arrived. Three big bulls were seen, and Roosevelt and his man went after them with all possible speed. They were on foot, and the trail led them over some soft ground, and then through a big patch of burnt timber. Here running was by no means easy, and more than once both hunters pitched headlong into the dirt and soot, until they were covered from head to foot. But Theodore Roosevelt was bound to get the elk, and kept on until the sweat was pouring down his face and neck. Shot after shot was fired, and all three of the animals were wounded, but still they kept on bounding away.

"One is down!" shouted Roosevelt at last. And the news proved true; the smallest of the bulls had rocked unsteadily for a few seconds and gone to earth. Then on and on after the remaining game sped the hunters, panting and sweating as before.

"The sweat streamed down in my eyes and made furrows in the sooty mud that covered my face, from having fallen full length down on the burnt earth," writes the dauntless hunter, in relating this story. "I sobbed for breath as I toiled at a shambling trot after them, as nearly done out as could well be."

But he did not give up; and now the elk took a turn and went downhill, with Theodore Roosevelt pitching after them, ready to drop from exhaustion, but full of that grit to win out which has since won the admiration of all who know the man. The second bull fell; and now but one remained, and this dashed into a thicket. On its heels went the daring hunter, running the chance of having the elk turn on him as soon as cornered, in which case, had Roosevelt's rifle been empty, the struggle for life on both sides would have been a fierce one.

In the midst of the thicket the hunter had to pause, for the elk was now out of sight, and there was no telling what new course had been taken by the game. At a distance he saw a yellow body under the evergreen trees, and, taking hasty aim, fired. When he came up, he was somewhat dismayed to learn that he had not brought down the elk, but a black-tail deer instead. In the meantime, the elk got away, and it proved impossible to pick up the trail again.

There is a valuable lesson to be learned from this hunting trip, and one that all young readers should take to heart. It shows what sticking at a thing can accomplish. Mr. Roosevelt had determined to get at least a portion of that game, no matter what the labor and hardship involved. Many a hunter would have given up in disgust or despair after the first few shots were fired and it looked as if the elk were out of range and intended to keep out. But this determined young man did not give up thus easily. Hard as was that run up hill and down, and regardless of the tumbles taken, and that he was so tired he could scarcely stand, he kept on until two elk were brought down, and it was firmly settled that the third could not be captured.

The way to accomplish anything in this life is to *stick at it*. Theodore Roosevelt understood this truth even when he went to college, for in the Harvard journal of which he was an editor he wrote, speaking of foot-ball practice, "What is most necessary is that every man should realize the necessity of faithful and honest work, *every afternoon*." He put "every afternoon" in italics himself, and he meant that every foot-ball player who hoped to win in the inter-collegiate foot-ball games should *stick at it* until he had made himself as perfect a player as possible. A victory worth gaining is worth working for, and usually the hardest-earned victories are the sweetest.

CHAPTER VIII

BRINGING DOWN A GRIZZLY BEAR BACK TO NEW YORK APPOINTED A CIVIL SERVICE COMMISSIONER THE WORK OF THE COMMISSION

It was while in the Bighorn Mountains that Theodore Roosevelt got his first shot at a bear. He had been wanting such a chance for a good many years, but up to that date the bears had kept well out of his sight.

In his writings he has said much about bears, both common and grizzly, and told of their habits, and how they have been tracked down and shot at various times of the year. He holds to the opinion that the average bear would rather run away than fight, yet he tells the story of how one bear faced the hunter who had shot him, and gave the man one blow with his powerful paw that proved fatal.

One day his companion of the hunt came riding in with the carcass of a black bear killed in a network of hollows and ravines some miles from their present camp.

"The hollows are full of bear tracks," said Merrifield. "I am sure, if we go up there, we'll get one or more black bears and perhaps a grizzly."

"Then let us go by all means," responded Theodore Roosevelt. And no time was lost in moving to the new locality.

The hunters had been out nearly all of the next day, when, on returning through the forest toward nightfall, Roosevelt came across the footmarks of a large bear. He tried to follow them, but night closed in on him, and he had to return to camp. That very night the bear came around the camp, looking for something to eat.

"Let us try to bring him down," cried Roosevelt, seizing his rifle, while his companion did the same. But outside it was pitch dark.

"Do you see him?" questioned Merrifield.

"No."

"Neither do I."

"Listen."

Both listened, and at a distance heard the bear lumbering off slowly through the woods. They went forward a short distance, then came to a halt.

"We'll have to give it up for the present," said Theodore Roosevelt. "But I am going to have him, sooner or later, if the thing is possible."

Early the next morning both of the hunters sallied forth and discovered that the bear had been at the carcasses of some game left in the forest. The tracks were fresh.

"He has been here, no doubt of it," said Merrifield. "Shall we wait for him to come again?"

"We might as well," was the answer. "He'll get hungry again, sooner or later."

So the pair sat down to watch. But the bear was shy, and kept his distance. Then it grew dark once more, so that but little could be seen under the trees.

"He knows enough to keep away," said Roosevelt's companion.

"Hark!" was the reply and both strained their ears. There was a faint crackling of twigs, and they felt certain it was the bear. But it was too dark to see anything; so both shouldered their rifles and walked back to camp.

Here was another illustration of Theodore Roosevelt's method of sticking at a thing. Two days had been spent in trying to get that bear, and yet he did not give up. On the following morning he sallied forth once more, as full of hope as before.

The bear had been at the carcass again, and the trail was now one to be followed with ease.

"I'm going to hunt him down to his lair," said Theodore Roosevelt, and stalked off with his companion beside him. Soon they were again deep in the woods, walking perhaps where the foot of white man had never before trod. Fallen trees were everywhere, and over these they often had to climb.

"Getting closer," whispered Roosevelt's companion, and pointed to some fresh claw scratches on the bark of fallen trees.

They now moved forward as silently as Indians, sure that the bear could not be far off. Suddenly Merrifield dropped on his knee as if to take aim. Roosevelt sprang to the front, with rifle raised. The bear was there, standing upright, only a few paces away. Without hesitation Theodore Roosevelt fired. His aim was true, and the great beast fell with a bullet straight between the eyes. The leaden messenger had entered his brain, and he died with scarcely a struggle.

"The whole thing was over in twenty seconds from the time I caught sight of the game," writes Mr. Roosevelt, in his book "Hunting Trips on the Prairies" (Part II of "Hunting Trips of a Ranchman"). "Indeed it was over so quickly that the grizzly did not have time to show fight at all or come a step toward me. It was the first I had ever seen, and I felt not a little proud as I stood over the great brindled bulk which lay stretched out at length in the cool shade of the evergreens. He was a monstrous fellow, much larger than any I have seen since, whether alive or brought in dead by hunters. As near as we could estimate he must have weighed about twelve hundred pounds."

There is a bear story for you, boys. And the best of it is, it is every word true. In later years Theodore Roosevelt brought down many more grizzlies, but I doubt if he was as proud of them as he was of that first capture.

While Theodore Roosevelt was spending a large part of his time in hunting and in literary work, and in studying political economy, Grover Cleveland's first term as President came to an end, and Benjamin Harrison was inaugurated to fill the office of Chief Magistrate.

At that time the question of Civil Service was again being agitated. Theodore Roosevelt was a warm advocate of the merit system, and knowing this, President Harrison appointed him, in 1889, a Civil Service Commissioner, and this office he held for six years, until his resignation in 1895. When Benjamin Harrison's term of office was up, and Grover Cleveland was reëlected to the Presidency, it was thought that Roosevelt would have to go, but his friend, the newly elected President, wished him to remain as a commissioner, and he did so for two years longer, thus serving both under a Republican and a Democratic administration.

To some of my young readers the term Civil Service, as applied here, may be a bit perplexing. For the benefit of such let me state that civil service here applies to the thousands of persons who work for the government, such as post-office clerks, letter carriers, clerks in the various departments at Washington, like the Treasury, the Congressional Library, the Government Printing Office, the War Department, and the hundred and one other branches in which Uncle Sam needs assistance.

For seventy or eighty years these various positions had been under what is commonly called the "spoils system." "To the victor belong the spoils," had been the old motto, which generally meant that the party happening to be in power could do as it pleased about dealing out employment to those under it. A worker might have been ever so faithful in the discharge of his duties, but if the administration was changed, he ran the risk of losing his position without any notice.

Statesmen of both great political parties had long seen the injustice of the spoils system, but few cared to take the matter up for fear of offending their political friends. But as matters grew worse, those who were honest said they would stand such a system no longer, and they began to advocate the merit plan, whereby each worker for our government should stand on his merit, so that he could not be removed from his position without just cause. This merit system is in operation to-day and is a most excellent thing, only becoming dangerous when extended too far.

There were two other commissioners besides Mr. Roosevelt on the Commission, but all worked together in harmony, although in many moves taken Mr. Roosevelt was the leader. About this work he has written a notable essay called "Six Years of Civil Service Reform," in which he reviews much of the work done. In this essay, among many other things, he says:

"No republic can permanently endure when its politics are corrupt and base; and the spoils system, the application in political life of the degrading doctrine that to the victor belong the spoils, produces corruption and degradation. The man who is in politics for the offices might just as well be in politics for the money he can get for his vote, so far as the general good is concerned." Certainly wise words and well worth remembering.

The work of the Commission was by no means easy, and the members were often accused of doing some things merely to benefit their own particular party or friends. Politicians of the old sort, who wanted everything they could lay hands on, fought civil service bitterly, and even those who might have been expected to help often held back, fearing they would lose their own popularity. Yet on the other hand, some members of Congress upheld the Commission nobly, and when President Garfield was assassinated by a half-crazy office-seeker many more came forward and clamored to put public offices on the merit system by all means.

Part of the work of the Commission was to prosecute the head of any bureau or department where an employee had been discharged or had suffered without just cause. Such cases came up in large numbers and were prosecuted with all the vigor of which the Commission were capable.

"We were not always successful in these trials," says Mr. Roosevelt. "But we won out in the majority of cases, and we gave the wrong-doing such a wide publicity that those who were guilty hesitated to repeat their actions." And he goes on to add that during his term of service not over one per cent. of those who worked for Uncle Sam were dismissed purely for political reasons. This was certainly an excellent record, and our government will do well to maintain such a high standard in the future.

To give a further idea of the work required in the way of examinations for positions under our government, let me state that during the year from July 1, 1890, to July 1, 1891, 5251 applicants were examined for the departments service, 1579 for the customs service, 8538 for the postal service, 3706 for the railway mail service, making a total of nearly 20,000, of which about 13,000 passed and the balance failed. Since our war with Spain, the work of the government has been vastly increased, and the places to be filled every year run up into figures that are startling.

One of the best and wisest acts of the Commission was to place the colored employees of the government on an equal footing with the white employees. In the past the colored employees had occupied their places merely through the whim or goodwill of those over them. Now this was changed, and any colored man who could pass the examination, and who was willing to attend strictly to his labor, was as safe in his situation as anybody.

CHAPTER IX

A Trip to the Shoshone Mountains Caught in a Driving Snowstorm Back to Work Resignation as Civil Service Commissioner

Notwithstanding the great amount of labor involved as a Civil Service Commissioner, Theodore Roosevelt did not forego the pleasures of the hunt, and in 1891 he made an extended trip to the Shoshone Mountains in Wyoming, going after elk and such other game as might present itself.

On this trip he was accompanied by his ranch partner, a skilled shot named Ferguson, and two old hunters named Woody and Hofer. There was also in the party a young fellow who looked after the pack-horses, fourteen in number.

The start was made on a beautiful day in September, and the party journeyed along at a gait that pleased them, bringing down everything that came to hand and which could be used as meat. Two tents were carried, one for sheltering their packs at night and the other for sleeping purposes.

In his book called "The Wilderness Hunter," Mr. Roosevelt has given many of the details of this grand hunt, which he says was one of the most exciting as well as most pleasurable undertaken. With an interest that cannot be mistaken, and which betrays the true sportsman at every turn, he gives minute descriptions of how the tents were erected, how everything in camp was put in its proper place, and how on wet days they would huddle around the camp-fire in the middle of the larger tent to keep warm and dry. He also tells how the packs on the horses were adjusted, and adds that the hunter who cannot take care of his outfit while on the hunt, or who must have all his game stalked for him, is a hunter in name only; which is literally true, as every genuine sportsman knows.

The young Civil Service Commissioner went out garbed in a fitting hunting costume, consisting of a buckskin shirt, with stout leggings, and moccasins, or, when occasion required, alligator-leather boots. Heavy overcoats were also carried and plenty of blankets, and for extra cold nights Theodore Roosevelt had a fur sleeping-bag, in which, no doubt, he slept "as snug as a bug in a rug."

The horses of a pack-train in the wild West are not always thoroughly broken, and although the majority rarely do anything worse than lag behind or stray away, yet occasionally one or another will indulge in antics far from desired. This was true on the present occasion, when at different times the pack-beasts went on a "shindy" that upset all calculations and scattered packs far and wide, causing a general alarm and hard work on the part of all hands to restore quietness and order.

For two days the hunters pushed on into the mountains with but little signs of game. Then a rain-storm set in which made the outlook a dismal one.

"Going to have a big storm," said one of the old hunters.

"Never mind, we'll have to take it as it comes," was Mr. Roosevelt's philosophical answer. "We can't expect good weather every day."

It was almost noon of that day when all heard the call of a bull elk, echoing over the hills. The sound came from no great distance, and in the face of the rain, Theodore Roosevelt and the hunter named Woody set off on foot after the beast, who was still calling as loudly as ever.

It was not long before the hunters could hear the bull plainly, as he pawed the earth, a challenge to another bull who was answering him from a great distance.

"We are gettin' closer to him," said Woody. "Got to go slow now, or he'll take alarm and be off like a flash."

The timber was rather thin, and the ground was covered with moss and fallen leaves, and over this the pair glided as silently as shadows, until Woody declared that the bull was not over a hundred yards away.

"And he's in a tearing rage, on account of that other bull," he added. "Got to plug him fair and square or there will be trouble."

Without replying to this, Theodore Roosevelt took the lead, keeping eyes and ears wide open for anything that might come to hand. Then through the trees he caught sight of the stately horns of the elk, as he stood with head thrown back, repeating his call in trumpet-like tones.

As the hunters came closer, the elk faced around and caught sight of his human enemies. Up went his antlers once more, as if to defy them.

"He's coming!" shouted Woody. And scarcely had he spoken when Theodore Roosevelt took aim and fired at the animal. There was a snort and a gasp, and the elk turned to run away. Then Roosevelt fired a second shot, and over went the monarch of the forest in his death agony. It was a fine bit of game to bring down, the antlers having twelve prongs. The head was cut off and taken back to camp, along with a small part of the best of the meat.

After that the forward march was resumed in the face of a sweeping rain that wet everybody to the skin. On they went until, just as the rain ceased, they reached a bold plateau, overlooking what is called Two-Ocean Pass, a wild and wonderful freak of nature, surrounded by lofty mountains and watered by streams and brooks flowing in several directions. Far up the mountains could be seen the snow-drifts, while lower down were the heavy forests and underbrush, the haunts of the game they were seeking.

In this Wonderland Theodore Roosevelt hunted to his heart's content for many days bringing down several more elk and also a fair variety of smaller game. It was now growing colder, and knowing that the winter season was close at hand, the hunters decided to strike camp and return homeward.

The movement was made none too soon. The snow was already filling the air, and one morning, on coming from his tent, Theodore Roosevelt found the ground covered to a depth of a foot and a half. To add to his discomfort the pony he was riding began to buck that day and managed to dislocate his rider's thumb. But Theodore Roosevelt stuck to him and showed him who was master; and after that matters went better. The snow continued to come down, and before the end of the journey was reached, at Great Geyser Basin, the hunters almost perished from the cold.

Such pictures as the above give us some idea of the varied life that Theodore Roosevelt has led. Even at this early age he was but thirty-three years old he had been a college student, a traveller, an author, an assemblyman, a ranchman and hunter, and a Civil Service Commissioner. He had travelled the length and breadth of Europe and through a large section of our own country. He had visited the palaces of kings and the shacks of the humble cowboys of the far West, he had met men in high places and in low, and had seen them at their best and at their worst. Surely if "experience is the school wherein man learns wisdom," then the future President had ample means of growing wise, and his works prove that those means were not neglected.

As already mentioned, when Grover Cleveland became President a second time, he requested Theodore Roosevelt to retain his place on the Civil Service Commission. This was a practical illustration of the workings of the merit system, and it made for Mr. Cleveland many friends among his former political enemies. By this movement the workings of the Commission were greatly strengthened, so that by the time Theodore Roosevelt resigned, on May 5, 1895, the Commission had added twenty thousand places filled by government employees to those coming under the merit system. This number was larger than any placed under the system before that time, and the record has scarcely been equalled since.

"He was a fighter for the system, day and night," says one who knew him at that time. "He was enthusiastic to the last degree, and had all sorts of statistics at his fingers' ends. If anybody in the government employ was doing wrong, he was willing to pitch into that person regardless of consequences. Some few politicians thought he was a crank on the subject, but the results speak for themselves. Some politicians, who wanted the old spoils system retained, were often after him like a swarm of angry hornets, but he never got out of their way, and when they tried to sting, he slapped them in a way that soon made them leave him alone. And more than that, he was very clever in the way that he presented his case to those representatives and senators who understood the real value of Civil Service reform. He made them appreciate what he and his fellow-commissioners were trying to do, and when the Commission was attacked in Congress it always had, as a consequence, a support that could not be easily overthrown."

When Theodore Roosevelt resigned, President Cleveland wrote as follows to him:

"You are certainly to be congratulated upon the extent and permanency of civil service reform methods which you have so substantially aided in bringing about. The struggle for its firm establishment and recognition is past. Its faithful application and reasonable expansion remain, subjects of deep interest to all who really desire the best attainable public service." It was high praise for the retiring commissioner, and it was well deserved.

CHAPTER X

APPOINTED POLICE COMMISSIONER OF NEW YORK CITY CORRUPTNESS OF THE DEPARTMENT STRENUOUS EFFORTS TO MAKE MATTERS BETTER A "DRY" SUNDAY ENFORCING THE TENEMENT HOUSE LAW AND OTHER MEASURES

During the time that Theodore Roosevelt was a Civil Service Commissioner there were several important political changes made in New York City.

In the past there had been a great deal of what is familiarly called "machine politics," and matters had been going from bad to worse. But now there was an upward turn by the election of William S. Strong to the office of mayor. Mr. Strong was a man of high character, and was elected by a vote that combined the best elements of all the political parties.

It was at a time when New York City was in urgent need of reform. Those in power were doing but little to stop the corruption that was stalking abroad upon every hand. Bribes were given and taken in nearly all departments, clerks were being paid large salaries for doing practically nothing, and contracts were put out, not to those who could do the best work, but to those who would pay the political tricksters the most money for them.

The record of the police department was perhaps the blackest of the lot. It was to this department that the citizens looked for protection from crime, yet it was known that many in the department winked at all sorts of vice, providing they were properly paid for so doing. Saloons and worse resorts were kept open in defiance of the law, and wickedness flaunted itself in the face of the public in a manner that was truly shocking. Occasionally a private citizen would try to do something to mend matters, but his complaint was generally "pigeon-holed," and that would be the end of the matter. The rottenness, as it was well called, extended from the highest places in the department to the lowest, so that it was said not even a policeman could secure his appointment without paying several hundred dollars for it, and this he was, of course, expected to get back by blackmailing those who lived or did business on his beat. And get it back the policeman would, even if he had to make an Italian fruit dealer pay him a dollar a month for having a stand on the sidewalk, where the walk was supposed to be free from obstruction.

When William Strong came into office, the first thing he did was to cast his eyes about him for reliable men who might aid him in purifying the city. He already knew of Theodore Roosevelt's work as an assemblyman and a Civil Service Commissioner.

"Mr. Roosevelt is just the man to take the office of Police Commissioner and put the department on an honorable basis," said the newly elected mayor, and he lost no time in tendering the office to Mr. Roosevelt. The tender was accepted, and Theodore Roosevelt was sworn into his new position on May 24, 1895.

The appointment of Mr. Roosevelt to the office of Police Commissioner was a great shock to nearly the entire police department. He was known for his sterling honesty, and it was felt that he would not condone crime in any shape or form.

"There will be a grand shaking up," said more than one. "Just you wait till he gets to the bottom of things. He'll turn the light on in a way that will make more than one officer tremble in his boots."

On the Board with Mr. Roosevelt were Andrew D. Parker, Avery D. Andrews, and Frederick D. Grant, the latter the son of former President Grant. Theodore Roosevelt was chosen president, and the Board lost no time in getting to work.

"The new Board found the department in a demoralized condition," says Mr. Roosevelt, in his report on the matter. "A recent grand jury had investigated the records of many officers, and many indictments had been found; 268 vacancies existed in the department, and 26 officers, including one inspector and five captains, were under suspension on account of indictment for crime." This was truly a sad state of affairs, and a horrible example to the other large cities of our Union.

The Commissioners went to work with a will, and Theodore Roosevelt was the leading spirit in every move made. Every branch of the police department was given an overhauling, and those who would not do their duty were promptly dismissed, while minor offences were met with heavy fines. By an act of the legislature the force of men was increased to eight hundred, to keep pace with the growth of the metropolis. The men who were particularly faithful in the discharge of their duties were rewarded by honorable mention, engrossed certificates, medals of honor, and by promotions. More than this, they were given to understand that if they did their duty faithfully they need not fear trouble from those over them, no matter what changes were made. No officer was allowed to accept blackmail money from those lower in the service; and above all, no politics were to interfere with the fair and square running of the whole department.

It was a gigantic task, and it cannot be said that it was totally successful, for the opposition in some quarters was strong. More than once Mr. Roosevelt was threatened with violence, but, as when an assemblyman, he paid but scant attention to these mutterings.

His habits of personally investigating matters still clung to him, and it is well remembered how he went around at odd hours of the day and night, and on Sundays, seeing if the policemen were really doing their duty. There had been a boast that all policemen were at their posts at night. Mr. Roosevelt went out once and found just two out of an even dozen where they should be. Then began that "shaking up" that has resulted in better police service in New York to this day.

The effect of the new vigor in the police department was felt in many other ways. There was a tenement-house law regarding buildings which were unfit for human habitations. New York City was crowded with such buildings, but nobody had ordered them torn down, because either nobody wanted to bother, or the owners paid blackmail money to keep them standing for the rent they could get out of them.

"Those tenements must come down," said Theodore Roosevelt.

"If you order them down, the owners will fight you to the bitter end," said another officer of the department.

"I don't care if they do. The houses are a menace to life and health. They are filthy, and if a fire ever started in them, some would prove regular traps. They have got to go." And shortly after that about a hundred were seized, and the most destroyed.

The enforcement of the Sunday liquor law was another thing that occasioned great surprise during Mr. Roosevelt's term as Police Commissioner. In the past, saloons had been almost as wide open on Sundays as on week days. On account of the cosmopolitan character of the population it was thought that to close up the saloons on Sundays would be impossible. But the police force was given strict orders, and on one Sunday in June, 1895, New York City had the first "dry" Sunday that it could remember in many years.

This "dry" Sunday provoked a new storm of opposition, especially from many of foreign birth, who were used to getting liquor as easily on that day as on any other. More threats were made against the vigorous commissioner, and on two occasions dynamite bombs were placed in his desk, evidently with the hope that they would explode and blow him to pieces. But the bombs were found in time, and no damage was done, and Theodore Roosevelt paid scant attention to them.

After that he was attacked in a new way. Some of the politicians laid traps for him whereby they hoped to bring discredit to his management of the department. The fight grew very hot and very bitter, and he was accused of doing many things, "just for the looks of them," rather than to benefit the public at large. But he kept on his way, and at last the opposition were silenced to such an extent that they merely growled behind his back.

For many years a large number of shiftless and often lawless men, and women too, were attracted to the metropolis because of the "Tramps' Lodging Houses" located there. These resorts were continually filled by vagrants who would not work and who were a constant menace to society at large.

"We must get rid of those lodging houses," said Mr. Roosevelt. "They simply breed crime. No respectable man or woman, no matter how poor, will enter them."

"But we'll have to have some sort of shelter for the poor people," said others.

"To be sure for those who are deserving. The others should be driven off and discouraged," answered Mr. Roosevelt. And one by one the tramps' lodging places were abolished. In their place the Board of Charities opened a Municipal Lodging House, where those who were deserving were received, were made to bathe, and given proper shelter and nourishment.

A story is told that, during the excitement attending the closing of saloons on Sunday, a friend came to Mr. Roosevelt and told about hearing some saloon-keepers plotting to harm him.

"What can they do?" demanded the Police Commissioner.

"I am afraid they can do a good deal," was the answer. "Each of those men has a barkeeper who has been in jail for various crimes. They may attack you some dark night and kill you."

"Perhaps I won't give them the chance," answered the man who had been on many a dangerous hunt in the wild West. "If they can shoot, so can I."

"But they may sneak up behind you and knock you out," insisted the visitor.

"Well, if they do that, I shall have died doing my duty," was the calm answer made by the future hero of the Rough Riders.

CHAPTER XI

APPOINTED FIRST ASSISTANT SECRETARY OF THE NAVY THE CONDITION OF AFFAIRS IN CUBA PREPARING FOR WAR THEODORE ROOSEVELT'S RESOLVE

While Theodore Roosevelt was serving as Police Commissioner of the city of New York, William McKinley ran for the Presidency of the United States the first time and was elected.

The young commissioner was a firm upholder of McKinley, for he did not believe in "free silver" as it was called, but in "sound money," which meant that in the future, as in the past, all national indebtedness should be made payable in gold, instead of in gold and silver, as many desired.

As soon as the new President was inaugurated, March 4, 1897, he appointed Hon. John D. Long to be Secretary of the Navy. Mr. Long knew Theodore Roosevelt well, and also knew of the "History of the Naval War of 1812," which the energetic author and commissioner had written.

"He is just the man we need here," said Mr. Long to President McKinley. "He has made a study of the navy, and he is not afraid of work," and without further delay Theodore Roosevelt was asked to resign his position in the metropolis and come to Washington, where he was duly installed as First Assistant Secretary of the Navy.

In his new position, certainly a high one for such a young man to occupy, Mr. Roosevelt had much to do. As first assistant, nearly the whole responsibility of the real workings of the department fell upon his shoulders. He took up these responsibilities manfully, and how well he succeeded in the work, history has abundantly proved.

"It was Roosevelt's work that made Dewey's victory at Manila possible," one who knew of the inner workings of the department has said, and another has said that the victory off Santiago Bay was also due in part to Roosevelt's watchfulness over the ships that took part in that conflict.

At Washington the Assistant Secretary found an era of extravagance equal to that which he had discovered in New York. The Navy Department was paying dearly for almost everything it bought, and many laborers and others were drawing high wages for doing little or no work. Against this Theodore Roosevelt set his face uncompromisingly, so that inside of a year the actual saving to our government was twenty-five per cent. When it is remembered that the Navy Department spends each year millions of dollars, something of what such a saving means can be realized.

For many years our country had been at peace with the whole world, but now a war cloud showed itself on the horizon, scarcely visible at first, but gradually growing larger and larger. Those at Washington watched it with great anxiety, wondering if it would burst, and what would be the result.

Cuba had been fighting for liberty for years. It was under Spanish rule, and the people were frightfully oppressed. To Spain they paid vast sums of money and got but little in return. Money that should have gone into improvements that should have supplied good roads and schools went into the pockets of the royalty of Spain. When a Cuban tried to remonstrate, he could scarcely get a hearing, and this state of affairs went from bad to worse until, in sheer desperation, the Cubans declared war on the mother-country, just as in 1776 our own nation threw off the yoke of England.

As my young readers know, Cuba lies only a short distance from the southeast coast of Florida. Being so close, it was but natural that our people should take an interest in the struggle at hand. Everybody sympathized with the Cubans, and some made offers of assistance. Then, when many Cubans were on the verge of starvation, we voted to send them relief in the way of something to eat.

The action of the United States was viewed with suspicion by Spain. The people of that country were certain we wanted to help Cuba only in order to "gobble her up afterward," as the saying went. Such was not our intention at all, and total Cuban liberty to-day testifies to that fact.

Not knowing how far matters might go, President McKinley and his advisers deemed it wise to prepare for the worst. This meant to put the army and navy on the best possible footing in the least possible time.

It was felt that should war come, it would be fought largely on the sea, and nobody realized this more than did Theodore Roosevelt. He was active day and night in the pursuit of his duty, seeing to it that this ship or that was properly manned, and this fortification and that put in proper order to resist attack. Our ships were in all parts of the world, on the Atlantic and the Pacific, in the far north and the far south, in European waters and Hong Kong Harbor. Each had to be supplied with coal and ammunition and with provisions. Those that were "out of commission," that is, laid up, generally for repairs, were put into commission with all speed. A thousand contracts had to be inspected, judged, and passed upon. Outwardly the Navy Department at Washington was moving along as peacefully as ever, internally it was more active than it had been at any time since the great Civil War.

"War may come at any moment," said Mr. Roosevelt to his friends. "And if it does come, there is nothing like being prepared for it."

About one thing Theodore Roosevelt was very particular. In the past, gun practice on board of our war-ships had been largely a matter of simply going through the motions of handling the guns.

"This will not do," said the Assistant Secretary. "Our gunners will never make good marksmen in that way. They must practise with powder and ball, shot and shell." And after that they did. Such practice cost a round sum of money, and the department was criticised for its wastefulness in this direction; but the worth of it was afterward proven when Commodore Dewey sank the Spanish ships in Manila Bay, and the Atlantic Squadron likewise destroyed the enemy's ships that were trying to escape from Santiago Harbor.

In those days at Washington, Theodore Roosevelt made a warm, personal friend of Dr. Leonard Wood. Dr. Wood was an army surgeon, who had seen considerable active service while under General Miles in the campaigns against the Apache Indians. Mr. Roosevelt has himself told how he and Dr. Wood would often, after office hours, take long walks out of the city, or play foot-ball, or go snow-skating when the weather permitted, and during such pastimes their conversation was invariably about the situation in Cuba, and what each intended to do should war break out.

"If war actually comes, I intend, by hook or by crook, to get out into the field," said Dr. Wood.

"I shall go with you," answered Theodore Roosevelt. "No more office work for me if there is any fighting to be done."

In the meantime, as already mentioned, matters in Cuba were rapidly approaching a crisis. Spain could not send a large enough army to the island to conquer the people while they were at liberty to roam through the jungles and mountains, and so began to drive men, women, and children into various cities or camps, where they were kept, under penalty of death if they tried to escape. Thus large numbers were torn from their homes, and sent miles and miles away, with no money, and nothing with which to support themselves. Food became scarce and high in price, and many grown folks and children were literally starved to death.

To help these starving people the Congress of our country voted to expend fifty thousand dollars from the national treasury. This excited Spain more than ever, and we were accused of trying to prolong the rebellion. But the deed was done, and many would have had us go farther, and recognize Cuba as a free and independent nation. This desire was overruled on the ground that our government could not with propriety endanger the peace of the world by taking so serious a step at that time. But the strength of popular sympathy with an oppressed people was shown by the fact that many Americans at grave personal risk went to Cuba, and joined the army in one capacity or another, fighting as bravely as if for their own individual rights.

CHAPTER XII

DESTRUCTION OF THE *MAINE* DEWEY'S VICTORY THEODORE ROOSEVELT BECOMES A SOLDIER ORGANIZING THE ROUGH RIDERS VARIOUS MEN IN THE COMMAND

"The *Maine* has been blown up!"

Such was the awful news which startled this whole nation in the middle of February, 1898, and which caused the question of war with Spain to crystallize without further deliberation.

The *Maine* was a battleship of large size, that had been sent down to the harbor of Havana, Cuba, on nothing more than a friendly visit. The explosion that destroyed this noble vessel occurred about ten o'clock at night, and was heard for miles around. Soon after the explosion, the war-ship began to sink, and over two hundred and fifty sailors and officers lost their lives.

The entire nation was now aroused, and many wanted to go to war with Spain immediately. But the Spaniards professed to be ignorant of the cause of the explosion, and said it must have come from the *inside* of the ship and not the *outside*. Without delay a Board of Inquiry was established, and it was settled that the explosion had come from the outside, probably from a mine set by the Spaniards in Havana Harbor.

"This means war, and nothing but war," said even the wisest of our statesmen. And so it proved. Without hesitation the whole nation sprang forward to uphold the administration, and in a few days Congress passed an appropriation of fifty millions of dollars "for national defence." It may be added that this appropriation was passed unanimously, regardless of party politics and regardless of the differences which, in the past, had existed between the North and the South.

We have already learned what had been done to prepare the navy for the conflicts to follow. Now there was even more work on hand, to get the army into shape for service in Cuba and on other foreign soil.

The regular army at that time consisted of about twenty-five thousand men, scattered all over the United States, on the frontier, at the Indian reservations, and along the sea-coasts. Many of these troops were hurried to camps in the southeast portion of our country, leaving but small garrisons in the far West.

It was realized by President McKinley that our regular army could not cope with the troubles at hand, and soon came a call for one hundred and twenty-five thousand volunteers. These volunteers were to come from the various States and Territories, each furnishing its proportion of soldiers according to its population. These soldiers were quickly collected and marched to the various state camps, there to be sworn into the service of the United States.

The "war fever" was everywhere, and many private parties began to raise companies, while all sorts of independent commands, Grand Army, Confederate Veterans, Italian-American Guards, German Singing Societies, Colored Guards, and the like, offered their assistance. Even the colleges caught the fever, and men went forth from Yale, Harvard, Princeton, and other institutions of learning to battle for Uncle Sam.

The first blow struck at Spain was a most effective one. Commodore, afterwards Admiral, Dewey was at Hong Kong when the trouble began, and he was directed by the War Department to hunt for a Spanish fleet somewhere among the Philippine Islands and engage it. On Sunday, May 1, came the news that the gallant commodore had reached Manila Bay, fought the Spanish fleet and sunk every hostile ship, and come out of the battle with all of his own ships safe and not a single man killed!

"Hurrah! that shows what our navy can do!" cried many citizens. And they were justly proud. In the past, foreign nations had looked with something akin to scorn on our vessels and the way they were manned. Now such criticism was silenced; and this result was, in a certain measure, due to the work of Theodore Roosevelt, while First Assistant Secretary to Secretary Long.

But Theodore Roosevelt was no longer in the department. He resigned and closed his desk, saying, "My duty here is done; my place is in the field." With such an active nature, it was impossible for him to remain a private citizen while stern war was a reality.

In his own excellent work, "The Rough Riders," and in his sworn testimony before the Commission of Investigation of the Spanish War, Mr. Roosevelt has given us graphic pictures of how the First United States Volunteer Cavalry, commonly called the Rough Riders, happened to be organized, and what it tried to do and did, and this testimony is supplemented by many who know the facts, and who took part in the battles which made the organization famous throughout the length and breadth of our land.

At first Theodore Roosevelt thought to attach himself to the militia of New York, but found every place taken.

"Let us try one of my Massachusetts regiments," said Dr. Wood. And this was also done, with a like result.

"We could fill every place, did we want five times as many men," said one colonel. "Everybody seems crazy to go." This shows how truly patriotic our nation can become when the occasion arises for going to the front.

While Theodore Roosevelt and his intimate friend were wondering what to do next, Congress authorized the raising of three cavalry regiments, to be composed of the daring riflemen and riders of New Mexico, Oklahoma, Arizona, and Indian Territory.

"There, that will just suit me," said Theodore Roosevelt. "I know many of those men, and I know we can raise a regiment in no time."

And without delay he sought out Secretary of War Alger and told him of his hopes.

"I am perfectly willing to give you command of one of those regiments," said the war secretary. "I know you are something of a rough rider yourself, and a good marksman to boot."

This was certainly flattering, but Theodore Roosevelt's head was not turned by the offer.

"I don't think I am quite ready to take command," said he. "I know that I can learn, and that quickly, but it will be precious time wasted."

"Well, what do you wish, Mr. Roosevelt?" asked the Secretary of War, curiously.

"What I should like best of all is for Dr. Wood to become colonel of the regiment, and for myself to become lieutenant-colonel."

"Very well; I will consult President McKinley on the subject," said the secretary. The request was granted, and in a few days more Colonel Wood and Lieutenant-Colonel Roosevelt sallied forth to organize the Rough Riders, and fit them for service in Cuba.

Leaving his family, which now consisted of his wife and six children, the lieutenant-colonel made his way to San Antonio, Texas, where the regiment was to gather. Previous to going he spent a full week in Washington, seeing to it that arrangements were completed for supplying the command with uniforms, carbines, saddles, and other articles which were needed. This was in itself quite a task, for all of the departments at the Capitol were more than busy, and it took a great amount of "hustling" to get what one wanted.

As soon as it was known that Theodore Roosevelt was going to help organize the Rough Riders, offers from everywhere began to pour in upon him. Not alone did the men of the plains and ranch who knew him want to go, but likewise his old college chums at Harvard. These men, of wealth and good families, were willing to serve in any capacity, if only they could be mustered in. There were crack base-ball and football players, yachtsmen, all-round athletes and men of fortune, all mixed in with hunters, cowboys, men who had served as sheriffs in the far West, where fighting was an everyday occurrence, some policemen who had served under Roosevelt when he was a Police Commissioner in New York, and even some Indians. Nearly every nationality was represented when it came to blood, and the men ran from the best educated to the most ignorant.

Theodore Roosevelt as a Rough Rider
(*Photograph by Pach Bros., N.Y.*)

But there were three tests which every man, private or officer, had to pass. He had to be in perfect health, he had to know how to ride, and he had to know how to shoot. To these conditions were afterward added two more: each man had to learn his duty as quickly as he could and had to learn to obey his superiors.

In such a collection of soldiers it was but natural that the real leaders soon asserted themselves. Several of the captains had served in the United States army before; two were former famous western sheriffs; and all were full of that pluck and energy which is bound to command success.

In this regiment were some men who had hunted with Theodore Roosevelt on more than one occasion. They knew him well and loved him, and did their best to serve him. To them he was really their commander, although they officially recognized Colonel Wood. They were preëminently "Roosevelt's Rough Riders," and the great majority of the people of our nation call them such to this day.

The majority of the command were rather young in years, although a few were of middle age. But all were tough and hardy, either from athletic training or from years spent in the open air of the great West. Some of them could ride almost any kind of a horse, and "bronco busting," that is, breaking in a wild steed, was common sport among them. Some had spent nearly their entire lives in the saddle, and some could exhibit remarkable skill with their firearms while riding at full speed.

When the men began to come into San Antonio, they found but little in the way of accommodations. But soon tents and blankets were procured. It is said that good shoes were scarce, but some of the soldiers did not mind going without them. The regiment was supplied with good rifles, but the cartridges were not made of smokeless powder, which was a bad thing, for smoke sometimes enables an enemy to locate the shooter, when, if smokeless powder were used, nothing could be seen. Each man had also a six shooter, and was to have had a machete, but the long knives did not come.

"On to Cuba!" was the cry. And it was taken up every day. The Rough Riders were eager for the fray. Alas! little did many of them realize that, once in the "bloody isle," they would never see their native land again.

CHAPTER XIII

IN CAMP AT TAMPA TO PORT TAMPA IN COAL CARS THEODORE ROOSEVELT'S QUICK MOVE TO OBTAIN A TRANSPORT THE WAIT IN THE HARBOR OFF FOR CUBA AT LAST

That the path of the soldier is not always one full of glory can easily be proven by what happened to the Rough Riders when, late in May, they were ordered to Tampa, Florida, where a part of the army was gathering in readiness to be transported to Cuba.

"We were just wild to go," says one of the number, in speaking of that time. "We were tired of staying at San Antonio and drilling day in and day out, rain or shine. I guess everybody felt like hurrahing when we piled on to the cars.

"Colonel Roosevelt he was only Lieutenant-Colonel then had six troops under him, and he did all he could to make the boys comfortable. But the cars were crowded, and travelling was so slow it took us four days to reach Tampa. Then when we got there, we found everything in confusion. The railroad yard was chock-a-block with freight and passenger cars, and nobody was there to tell us where to go or where to find provisions.

"The boys were hungry and tired out, for sleeping on the railroad had been almost out of the question. There wasn't a sign of rations in sight, and it looked as if we would have to stay hungry. But Teddy Roosevelt just put his hand into his own pocket and bought us about all we wanted. Then he scurried around and found out where we were to go, and in another twenty-four hours we were settled in camp." Even in camp the Rough Riders had to put up with continued discomfort. The weather was warm, flies and mosquitoes were numerous, and the drinking water was not of the best.

The rations were plain, but the Rough Riders did not mind this, for many of them had often fared worse on the plains.

Although it was now a regular military camp that the Rough Riders were in, it was rather difficult to control some of the men, especially those who had been used to an unusually rough life. But they were held in check as much as possible by their commanders, and on Sunday all attended a church service held by Chaplain Brown, who spoke to them in a manner that soon claimed their attention.

After but a few days spent in the camp at Tampa, within walking distance of many of the fashionable hotels, the command was ordered to Port Tampa, there to board a transport to sail for some destination not revealed. But the soldiers knew they were going to Cuba, to fight the Spaniards and to aid in freeing Cuba, and again there was a loud hurrahing.

But immediately on top of this came one of the hardest blows the Rough Riders had to endure, and one which some of them will probably never forget.

As already stated, volunteers from all over our nation were anxious to get into the fight, and it was no easy matter for the authorities at Washington to decide who should go and who should be left behind.

"Only eight troops of seventy men each of the Rough Riders will embark on the transport," was the order sent to Colonel Wood. More than this, it was ordered that the command should be on board of the transport by the following morning, otherwise it could not go.

"Four troops to be left behind!" exclaimed Theodore Roosevelt.

"Too bad," returned Colonel Wood. "Every man expects to go, and wants to go."

It was a hard task to tell some of the men that they could not go. Mr. Roosevelt tells us that many of them actually cried at the news. They were willing to go under any conditions. They did not want any pay, they did not want any pensions if they were disabled, and some, who had money, even offered to pay their way, just for the privilege of fighting for Uncle Sam. After such an exhibition, let nobody dare to say that true patriotism is dying out in this country.

But orders were orders, and as quickly as possible those to go were selected. Then the command marched to the railroad tracks to await the cars. None came, and they were given orders to march to another track. This they also did; but still no train appeared.

"We'll be left, that is certain," said Colonel Wood, anxiously.

"It certainly looks like it, unless we march the boys down to the port."

"Here comes a train!" was the cry.

It was a train, but only of empty coal cars. It was about to pass by when the Rough Riders halted it.

"What's the matter with riding down to the port in the coal cars?" was the question asked by several.

"Good enough!" came the answer. "Into the cars, boys, and don't waste time!" And into the dirty coal cars they piled, and persuaded the engineer of the train to take them down to Port Tampa as quickly as he could.

If there had been bustle and confusion up at Tampa, it was far worse at the port. Everybody was in a hurry, and ten thousand soldiers stood around, not knowing what to do with their baggage, and not knowing which of the many transports to board.

At last the Rough Riders were told to go aboard the *Yucatan*, and started to do so.

"The *Yucatan*?" exclaimed a member of another command. "That is our transport."

"No, she has been allotted to us," put in an officer belonging to still another command.

"How many men will she hold?" questioned a captain of the Rough Riders.

"About a thousand."

"Then she can't take the three commands."

Theodore Roosevelt overheard this talk, and at once made up his mind that it would be a question of what command got aboard of the transport first. Without the loss of a moment he ran back to where his men were in waiting.

"Double-quick to the dock!" was his order. And forming quickly, the troops made their way to the wharf with all possible speed. In the meantime, Colonel Wood had gone out to the transport in a steam-launch and gotten the vessel to come up to the wharf. On board went the Rough Riders pell-mell, and not a minute too soon.

"This is our boat!" cried an officer, as he came up with his command a minute later.

"Sorry for you, sir, but it is our boat," was Colonel Wood's firm answer.

Then the third command loomed up, and a three-handed dispute arose. But the Rough Riders remained aboard of the transport, taking four companies of another command in with them.

I have told of the particulars of this affair to show my young readers what was needed at this time, and how well Theodore Roosevelt performed his duties. He had been a soldier and officer only a few weeks, yet he realized that army life on paper and army life in reality were two different things. He felt that an officer must do much besides leading his men in the field: that he must look after them constantly, see that their health was provided for, see that they got their rations, see that transportation was ready when needed, and even see to it that some were kept away from the temptations of drink, and that they did not quarrel among themselves.

When going on board of the transport, the Rough Riders were supplied with twelve days' rations each. The most of the food was good, but the canned beef was very bad, just as it was found to be very bad in many other quarters, and it made a great number sick. Added to this, somebody had forgotten to issue salt to the soldiers; so much had to be eaten without this very necessary seasoning.

"But we took matters good-naturedly," said one of the number, in speaking of the trip that followed. "Many of the boys were out for a lark, and when they growled, they did it good-naturedly. We had all sorts of men, and all sorts of nicknames. An Irishman was called Solomon Levi, and a nice young Jew Old Pork Chop. One fellow who was particularly slow was called Speedy William, and another who always spoke in a quick, jerky voice answered to the hail of 'Slow-up Peter.' One cowboy who was as rough as anybody in the command was christened The Parson, and a fine, high-toned, well-educated college boy had to answer to the name of Jimmy the Tramp. Some of the boys could sing, and they organized the Rough Rider Quartette; and others could play, and they gave us music on the mouth harmonicas and other instruments they had managed to smuggle along."

The War Department had expected to send the troops to Cuba without delay, but now came in a report that some Spanish war-ships were hovering around, ready to sink the transports as soon as they should show themselves, and for five days the vessels remained in Port Tampa Harbor, until it was ascertained that the report was untrue.

Those five days were important to Theodore Roosevelt and to the men under him. Every day the young officer spent a certain portion of his time in studying military tactics and in drilling his soldiers. Much had still to be learned, and the officers had their school of instructions as well as did those under them.

The weather was broiling hot, and some were already suffering from fever or its symptoms. Fortunately bathing was good, and many went in once or twice a day. Bathing in the ocean was great sport to some of the plainsmen who had never seen anything larger than a river or creek, and they frolicked around like children, and got up races, with prizes for the best swimmers.

At last came the orders for the transports to set sail for Cuba. They numbered thirty-two in all, including a schooner which was towed along filled with drinking water, for water must be had, and that was the only place where it could be stowed. To protect the transports from a possible attack by the enemy, they were accompanied by five war-ships at first, and later on by fourteen. All told, there were on the transports eight hundred officers and sixteen thousand enlisted men. Of the commands, the most were from the regular army, the volunteers numbering but three the Rough Riders, the Seventy-first New York Infantry, and the Second Massachusetts Infantry.

CHAPTER XIV

LIFE ON THE TRANSPORT THE LANDING AT DAIQUIRI THE MARCH TO SIBONEY THE TRAIL THROUGH THE JUNGLE THE SKIRMISH AT LA GUASIMA

While the army was preparing to invade Cuba, matters so far as they concerned the navy had been moving along rapidly. Commodore Dewey had sunk the Spanish fleet in Manila Bay; Havana and the adjacent coasts were being blockaded, so no ships could pass in or out without running the risk of capture; and a large fleet of war-ships under Admiral Cervera, of the enemy's navy, had been "bottled up" in Santiago Harbor.

It had been decided that the United States troops should be landed on the southeast coast of Cuba, not far from the entrance to Santiago Bay, and from that point should make an advance on Santiago, which is the second city of importance in the island.

Day after day the flotilla of transports kept on its way, spread out in a broad column during the time it was light, and coming in close together during the night. The war-ships hovered near, and at night swept the ocean with their powerful search-lights, rendering a surprise by the enemy impossible.

The trip to the southeast coast of Cuba lasted seven days. It was very hot, even for this time of the year, and those who could, slept on deck during the voyage. There was but little to do, and when not drilling, the men took it easy in the shade, sleeping, chatting, or playing games. Sometimes they would talk of the future and wonder how much of real fighting lay before them.

"We didn't know even then where we were going," said one, in speaking of the trip. "I don't believe Wood or Roosevelt knew either. First we thought it might be Havana, then we imagined it might be Porto Rico, but when we turned southward and ran around the eastern end of the island, we all knew we were bound for Santiago."

As the transports swept up toward the mouth of Santiago Bay, they came within sight of the American war-ships that were keeping Admiral Cervera's fleet "bottled up" in the harbor. A shout of recognition went up, and one of the bands struck up a patriotic air that was truly inspiring.

The landing of the Rough Riders and many other commands was made at Daiquiri, a small settlement on the coast east of Santiago Harbor. The *Yucatan* got closer to the shore than most of the other transports, and the men lost no time in disembarking, taking with them two Colt's automatic guns and a dynamite gun of which they had become possessed. As there had not been transports enough, only the officers' horses had been brought along. These were thrown into the water and made to swim ashore. Theodore Roosevelt had two horses, but one was drowned.

It was important that the landing should be guarded, and the war-ships sent in some shot and shell to dislodge any Spaniards who might be in the vicinity. But none showed themselves, and soon nearly all of the soldiers were ashore, either at Daiquiri or at a landing a short distance farther westward. No enemy was in sight, and the only persons who appeared were some Cubans, soldiers and civilians, who wanted but one thing, food.

The Rough Riders had been put into a brigade commanded by General S.B.M. Young. There were two of these brigades, and it is worth noting that they formed a division under the command of Major-General Joseph Wheeler, who had in years gone by fought so gallantly on the side of the

Confederacy. Now, as brave as of old, he was fighting for Old Glory, the one banner of the North and the South alike.

As the Rough Riders landed, they were marched up the beach, and here they went into temporary camp, an easy matter, since each soldier carried his outfit with him, or, at least, as much as he could get of what belonged to him. Theodore Roosevelt had his weapons and ammunition, a mackintosh and a toothbrush, certainly much less than he had carried even when roughing it in the Bad Lands of the West.

As soon as the larger portion of the army was landed, General Lawton he who was afterward to give his life for his flag in the Philippines threw out a strong detachment on the Santiago road to the westward, and also detachments on the roads to the north and east.

"On to Santiago!" was the cry. And many were for pushing forward without delay. But the transports had still to unload their baggage, and word did not reach the Rough Riders to move on until the afternoon of the day after landing.

It was a rocky, uneven country, with much brushwood and jungles of trees and vines. It had rained, but now the sun came out fiercely, and the Rough Riders (riders in name only, for only the officers were on horseback) suffered greatly through being clad in winter uniform.

"It was a tough and tiresome march," said one who was there. "The air just quivered with heat, and many of the boys felt like throwing half of their clothing away. Whenever we reached a drinking place, the crowd would swarm around for water like a lot of bees.

"General Lawton had his outposts pretty well advanced. Our commander, old General Wheeler, was just as anxious to make a showing, and he ordered General Young to push on with the Rough Riders and some other troops. So away we went, with Colonel Wood at our head, and Lieutenant-Colonel Roosevelt in command of one squadron and Major Brodie in command of the other. In some spots the road was frightful, full of mud-holes, with big land crabs crawling around in all directions, and with the trailing vines full of poisonous spiders. We didn't know but that the woods might be full of Spaniards, and we were on the alert to give the Dons as good as they sent, should they show themselves."

By nightfall the Rough Riders reached the little village of Siboney without having met the enemy. Here they went into camp in the midst of a heavy thunder-storm in which every soldier and officer was drenched to the skin. Fires could scarcely be lighted, and it was not until the storm had partly cleared away that the cooks could prepare anything to eat. Surely being a soldier was not all glory after all.

It had been learned that a portion of the Spanish army was less than four miles away, and General Young was ordered by General Wheeler to move forward at daybreak and engage the enemy. Colonel Wood received orders to move the Rough Riders by a trail over a hill, beyond which the country sloped toward the bay and the city of Santiago.

The first encounter with the enemy occurred at a place called La Guasima (or Las Guasimas), so called on account of trees of that name growing in the vicinity. Here the Spaniards had rifle-pits and mounds of earth to shelter them and had likewise the sugar-house of a plantation. They had been watching for the coming of the *Americanos* eagerly, and were determined to give our soldiers a lesson not to be forgotten. They knew that our army had not been in active warfare for years, and felt certain that they would soon be able to make the "paper" soldiers retreat.

The Rough Riders found the way led up a steep hill, and the pace was so fast that before the firing line was reached some men fell out from exhaustion. Theodore Roosevelt was at the head of the first squadron and did his best to urge those under him forward. There was an advance guard, led by some men under Sergeant Hamilton Fish, and Captain Capron's troop, and soon a crash of firearms notified all that a fight was on.

Orders were at once issued to fill the magazines of the guns, and this was done. Then, while some troops moved to the left of the trail, Lieutenant-Colonel Roosevelt was ordered to take three troops to the right. Here the jungle was heavy, and no sooner had the Rough Riders advanced than the Spaniards opened fire upon them. In speaking of the opening of this fight, Mr. Roosevelt himself writes:

"The effect of the smokeless powder (used by the enemy) was remarkable. The air seemed full of the rustling sound of the Mauser bullets, for the Spaniards knew the trails by which we were advancing, and opened heavily on our position. But they themselves were entirely invisible. The jungle covered everything, and not the faintest trace of smoke was to be seen in any direction, to indicate from whence the bullets came."

It was certainly a trying time to stand up and be shot at without being able to return the compliment. Roosevelt and all the other leaders knew that this would not do, and at a great risk they continued to advance, until some Spaniards were at last discovered across a valley to the right of where the troops under Lieutenant-Colonel Roosevelt were located.

"There they are!" was the cry. "Forward and at 'em, boys! Down with the Dons!" Without delay some sharpshooters fired on the Spaniards, and then the regular troops opened up, and at last the Spaniards ran from cover.

Bullets were now flying in all directions, and both sides were making their shots tell. The Americans had but scant protection, and it was not long before a number of them fell. Some bullets came close to Theodore Roosevelt, and one hit a palm tree near where he was standing, filling his left eye and ear with the dust and splinters. Had that Mauser bullet come a few inches closer, the man who was destined to become the future President of our country might have been killed on the spot.

In the midst of the skirmish for the conflict proved to be nothing more there was a report that Colonel Wood was dead, and Theodore Roosevelt took it upon himself to restore the fighting line of Rough Riders to order. But happily the report proved false; and a little while after this the skirmish came to an end, and both Spaniards and Americans betook themselves to positions of greater safety. In this skirmish, brief as it was, the Rough Riders lost eight men killed and nearly forty wounded.

CHAPTER XV

ALONG THE JUNGLE TRAIL FORDING THE RIVER OPENING OF THE BATTLE OF SAN JUAN HILL BRAVERY OF THE ROUGH RIDERS PERSONAL EXPERIENCES OF THEODORE ROOSEVELT DURING THE BATTLE

Taken as a whole, the skirmish at La Guasima was quite an important one, for it showed the Spaniards that our soldiers were bound to advance upon Santiago, be the cost what it might.

More than this, it showed that Theodore Roosevelt was brave under fire. During the skirmish he paid but scant attention to his own personal safety. He went wherever he thought he was needed, and the fact that Mauser bullets were flying about in all directions did not daunt him.

"He was about as cool a man as I ever saw in a fight," said one old soldier. "He did all he could to encourage the men, and had a kind word for every man he ran across who was wounded. Once, in the thickest of the brush, he grabbed up a gun and began to shoot with us, and I reckon he fired as straight as anybody there, for he had had lots of practice while hunting."

The Spaniards had been driven from their pits and from the sugar-house of the plantation, and now took good care to keep out of sight. Picket-guards were thrown out by the officers of the army, and those who had been in the fight took a much-needed rest, and looked after the dead and wounded. There was certainly a touching scene at the temporary hospital, where one soldier started to sing "My Country, 'tis of Thee," and many others joined in. On the following morning the dead were buried, the men gathering around the one common grave to sing "Rock of Ages" in a manner that brought tears to the eyes of many.

From La Guasima the Rough Riders moved to the bank of a small stream in the neighborhood. Part of the army was ahead of them and the rest behind, and for several days nothing unusual occurred. But during that time General Young caught the fever, whereupon Colonel Wood had to take charge of the brigade, and Lieutenant-Colonel Roosevelt took command of the Rough Riders.

It was now the end of June, and the weather was anything but agreeable. When the rain did not come down in torrents, the sun shone with a glare and a heat that was terrific. As said before, the uniforms of the Rough Riders were heavy, and much clothing had to be cast aside as unfit for use. To add to the discomfort, rations that were promised failed to appear, so that a good square meal was almost unknown.

"This will not do; the men must have enough to eat, even if I have to buy it for them," said Acting Colonel Roosevelt, and made two trips down to the seacoast in search of beans, tomatoes, and other things to eat. Here he was informed that he could only buy stuff meant for the officers.

"All right; I'll buy the things for the officers," he answered, and purchased as much as they would allow. When he got back, he turned the food over to the officers, but saw to it that they gave their men a fair share.

"It was a kindness none of his men ever forgot," said a soldier who was there. "It wasn't any of his business to buy the grub, the commissary department had to supply it free, but he knew we might starve while the department was getting itself straightened out and ready to do the right thing. Before he went on a hunt for food, all we had was salt pork, hardtack, and coffee, and some of the stuff wasn't fit to put in your mouth." And this testimony was the testimony of scores of others.

The Spaniards were strongly intrenched upon the outskirts of Santiago, and as it was a rough, hilly country, with many shallow streams and much jungle, it was hard for the American army to advance. It was General Shafter's idea to form a grand semicircle around Santiago, starting from El Caney on the north, and running in an irregular line to Aguadores on the south. Throughout this territory the Spaniards had done everything possible to hinder the advance of our troops. Barbed wire was strung in many directions, and often the brushwood would conceal dangerous pitfalls, so that any advance had to be made with great caution.

The attack upon the Spanish lines began on July 1, and the fighting took place in several quarters at once, but was unusually heavy at El Caney and at San Juan Hill. At El Caney the heroic General Lawton was in command, and fought as gallantly as he afterward did in the Philippines. Some of the charges were terrific, and will ever be remembered by those who participated in them.

The Rough Riders struck camp and moved along the trail on the last day of June. It was as hot as ever, with no sign of rain. The trail was filled with troops and provision wagons, and the progress, consequently, was slow.

"Let us get into the fight!" was the cry heard on every side. "Don't keep us waiting any longer."

"Keep cool," said one of the officers. "You'll get all the fighting you want soon." And so it proved.

At a little after eight o'clock in the evening the Rough Riders found themselves on El Poso Hill, and here the whole brigade to which they were attached went into camp.

"It wasn't much of a camp," said one who was there. "We just threw out a strong picket-guard and went to sleep on our arms, and glad of it, after that day in the broiling sun. We had had to ford some pretty muddy streams, and all of us were water and mud up to our knees. But everybody was as enthusiastic to fight as ever."

At sunrise the battle opened at El Caney, and the Rough Riders could hear the booming of cannon. At once all was activity, and the men prepared to move ahead at a moment's notice.

Acting Colonel Roosevelt was with Colonel Wood at the time, and both were listening to the roar of the artillery.

"I wish we could move " began Colonel Wood, when, of a sudden, both he and Theodore Roosevelt heard a strange humming sound in the air. Then came the explosion of a shrapnel shell over their heads, and both leaped to their feet.

"This is getting warm!" cried Theodore Roosevelt, and ran toward his horse, when boom! came another explosion, and one of the bullets fell upon his wrist, making, as he himself says, "a bump about as big as a hickory nut." This same shell, he adds, wounded four of the men under him and two or three regulars, one of whom lost his leg. Certainly another providential escape on the part of the future President.

Without loss of time Theodore Roosevelt ordered his troops into the underbrush, and here, for the time being, they were safe. On account of the smokeless powder they used, the

Spanish batteries could not be precisely located, so our own artillery were at a slight disadvantage.

But now the blood of the Americans was fully aroused, and soon came an order for a general advance, something that was hailed with wild delight by the Rough Riders.

"Hurrah, now we'll show 'em what the Yankees can do!" was the cry. "Down with the Dons! Three cheers for Uncle Sam!"

The Rough Riders had to ford the river, and while they were doing this, a balloon that had been used for observations came down in that vicinity and attracted the attention of the Spanish sharpshooters. The firing was now heavy on all sides, and many a gallant soldier went down to rise no more.

Then came another wait of an hour, during which the Rough Riders rested in a hollow leading up from the river. Again there was grumbling. With so much fighting on all sides, why could they not advance?

"We'll get our turn," said Theodore Roosevelt. And soon after a staff officer dashed up with orders to move forward and support the cavalry of the regular army on the hills in front.

"Now to the front!" was the cry. "Down with the Dons!" And away went troop after troop on the double-quick, with Acting Colonel Roosevelt leading them. Shot and shell were hurling themselves through the air in all directions, and on all sides could be heard the shrieks and groans of the dead and the dying. It was a time long to be remembered. Men went down in all directions, and with them not a few officers. It was so hot that Roosevelt's orderly was prostrated from the heat and afterward died. Roosevelt summoned another Rough Rider, and had just finished giving the man some orders when the soldier pitched forward upon his commander, killed by a bullet through the throat.

As the troops advanced, Theodore Roosevelt urged his men forward and told them to do their best, to which they responded with a cheer. He was on horseback at the time, and soon came across a man lying in the shade, probably overcome by the heat. He started to speak to the Rough Rider when a bullet hit the fellow and killed him on the spot.

"I suppose that bullet was meant for me," says Mr. Roosevelt, in writing of this incident. "I, who was on horseback in the open, was unhurt, and the man lying flat on the ground in the cover beside me was killed."

The fight had now centred around the possession of San Juan Hill, upon which was located a Spanish blockhouse. The bullets were flying as thickly as ever, when Roosevelt was ordered to advance in support of another regiment. As the Rough Riders reached the spot where the other regiment was, they found the men lying down awaiting orders.

"I am ordered to support your regiment," said Theodore Roosevelt to the first captain he met.

"We are awaiting orders to advance," answered the captain of the regulars.

"In my opinion we cannot take these hills by firing at them," returned the commander of the Rough Riders. "We must rush them."

"My orders are to keep my men where they are."

"Where is your Colonel?"

"I don't know."

"Well, if he isn't here, then I am the ranking officer, and I give the order to charge," came quickly and positively from Theodore Roosevelt.

"Well, sir, I I have orders from our Colonel " began the captain of the regulars.

"If you won't charge, let my men pass through, sir," cut in the Acting Colonel of the Rough Riders, and he ordered his men to move to the front. This was too much for the regulars, and up they sprang with shouts and yells, and Rough Riders and regulars went up San Juan Hill together. Roosevelt was on horseback as before, but at a barbed-wire fence he leaped to the ground, swung his hat in the air, and joined his men on foot.

The fight was now at its fiercest, and men were being mowed down in all directions. But the fever of battle was in the veins of all the American soldiers, and nothing could stop them. Up the hill they went, loading and firing at random, and making as many shots as possible tell. The Spaniards were in retreat, and soon Old Glory was planted in several places. Some of the leading officers had been shot, and Theodore Roosevelt found himself at one time in command of five regiments, and doing his best to keep them in military order. Strange as it may seem, with bullets flying all around him, he remained unharmed, saving for some slight scratches which, he tells us, "were of no consequence."

With the top of the hill gained, the American soldiers could get a distant glimpse of Santiago, several miles away, and some wanted to move still farther forward. But the Spaniards had strong intrenchments to fall back upon, and it was deemed best to "let well enough alone." Accordingly the American line was made as strong as possible, and by nightfall the battle was at an end, and the Rough Riders were told to hold the hill and intrench, and they did so. In the blockhouse they found some food belonging to some Spanish officers, and upon this they feasted after their well-earned victory.

CHAPTER XVI

RESULTS OF THE FIGHT LIFE IN THE TRENCHES THE SPANISH FLEET IN SANTIAGO HARBOR ANOTHER GREAT NAVAL VICTORY THE ROUGH RIDERS AND THE SPANISH GUERILLAS

The fight had been a hard and heavy one. The Rough Riders had gone into the engagement just 490 strong, and of that number 89 were killed or wounded. The total loss to the Americans was 1071 killed and wounded. The loss to the Spanish was also heavy, but the exact figures will probably never be known.

Utterly tired out with their marching and fighting, the Rough Riders intrenched as best they could, cared for their wounded and dead, and then dropped down to get a well-earned rest. The night was misty and cold, and many who had been bathed in perspiration suffered accordingly. Theodore Roosevelt had a blanket taken from the Spanish, and in this he rolled himself, and slept with others of his command.

At three o'clock in the morning came an unexpected alarm. The Spanish skirmishers were out in force, trying to drive the Americans back. But there was no heavy attack, and presently all became as quiet as before.

"They'll not give up yet," said one of the officers of the Rough Riders. "They mean to retake this hill if they can."

Just at daybreak the Spaniards opened the attack on San Juan Hill once more. Theodore Roosevelt was resting under a little tree when a shrapnel shell burst close by, killing or wounding five men of the command. He at once ordered the eight troops under him to a safer position, where the Spanish battery and the sharpshooters could not locate them so readily.

If the fight had been hard, guarding the trenches was almost equally so. The sun beat down fiercely, and the newly turned up earth made many of the Rough Riders sick. Added to this, provisions were, as usual, slow in arriving. Those in the trenches were kept there six hours, and then relieved by the others who were farther to the rear.

"Running from the cover of brush to the trenches was no easy matter," says one Rough Rider who was there. "We had dug the trenches in a hurry, and had no passages from the rear leading to them. All we could do was to wait for a signal, and then rush, and when we did that, the Spaniards would open a hot fire and keep it up for perhaps fifteen minutes. The sun was enough to turn a man's brain, and more than one poor fellow caught a fever there that proved fatal to him."

Through the entire day the firing continued, but no advances were made upon either side. The Americans were waiting for reinforcements, and the Spaniards were doing likewise. On our side a dynamite gun and two Colt's guns were used, but with little success. But the Gatling guns proved very effective, and caused a great loss to the enemy.

The city of Santiago lies on the northeast coast of a large bay of the same name. This bay is shaped somewhat like a bottle, with a long neck joining it to the Caribbean Sea.

In the harbor, at the time of the battles just described, the Spaniards had a fleet of war-ships under the command of Admiral Cervera, an old and able naval commander. In the fleet were four large cruisers and two torpedo-boats. Three of the cruisers were of seven thousand tons burden each, and all could make from eighteen to nineteen knots an hour. Each carried a crew of about five hundred men, and all were well supplied with guns and ammunition.

To keep this fleet "bottled up," our own navy had a fleet of its own just outside of the harbor, where it had been stationed ever since Admiral Cervera had been discovered within. The American fleet consisted of the cruiser *Brooklyn*, which was Commodore Schley's flag-ship, the battleships *Texas*, *Iowa*, *Indiana*, and *Oregon* (the latter having sailed all the way from the Pacific coast around Cape Horn to get into the fight), and the converted yachts *Gloucester* and *Vixen*. There were also close at hand, but not near enough to get into the fight, the cruiser *New York*, Admiral Sampson's flag-ship, and several other vessels of lesser importance.

For a long time it had been thought that Cervera would try to escape from the harbor, in which he could not be reached because of the strong forts that protected the entrance. To bottle him up more effectively, the Americans tried to block up the harbor entrance by sinking an old iron steamboat, the *Merrimac*, in the channel. This heroic work was undertaken by Lieutenant Hobson with a crew of seven daring men, but the plan failed, for the *Merrimac*, instead of sinking where intended, swung to one side of the main channel.

When it was reported to him that the Americans had taken the heights of El Caney and San Juan and were strongly intrenched in their positions, Admiral Cervera concluded that Santiago Bay might soon become too hot to hold him. The capture of the city would be followed by the taking of the forts at the harbor entrance, and then there would be nothing left for him to do but to surrender.

San Juan and El Caney had been taken on Friday, and all day Saturday occurred the shooting at long range, as already described. In the meantime the war-ships outside of the harbor kept up a close watch on the harbor entrance, lying well out during the day, but coming in closer at night, and using their powerful search-lights from sundown to sunrise.

Sunday dawned bright and clear, and for the time being all was quiet both ashore and afloat. In the trenches the Rough Riders and other soldiers were still on guard, doing what they could for their wounded, and trying to get the rations which were still delayed.

Presently, those on board of the American fleet noticed a thick cloud of smoke hanging over the harbor, coming from the funnels of the Spanish war-ships. Then one of the enemy's vessels showed itself, quickly followed by the others, and all turned westward, to escape up the coast.

"The enemy is escaping!" was the signal hoisted. And then one cannon after another boomed out, giving the signal to all our ships in that vicinity. The booming of the cannon was heard away eastward at Siboney, whither Admiral Sampson had gone with his ship to confer with General Shafter, and without delay the *New York* raced madly back to get into the fight that followed.

"Remember the *Maine!*" was the cry. "Down with the Spanish ships! Give 'em what Dewey did!" And this cry, "Give 'em what Dewey did!" was heard on every hand.

The first vessel to go down was a torpedo-boat, sunk by the *Gloucester*, and this was quickly followed by the sinking of the second torpedo-boat. In the meantime the larger vessels were pouring in their rain of steel upon the Spanish cruisers with deadly effect, knocking great holes into the ships and killing scores of those on board.

The Spanish cruiser *Teresa* was the first to succumb to the heavy attack, and soon she turned in to shore to save her crew from drowning. Then the *Oquendo* caught fire in several places, and burning fiercely from stem to stern, she, too, turned in.

But two ships were now left to Admiral Cervera, the *Vizcaya* and the *Colon*, and each had suffered much. Both were doing their best to get out of reach of our guns and the marvellous accuracy of our gunners.

"Don't let 'em get away!" was the cry. "Give 'em what Dewey did!" Forward went the war-ships of Uncle Sam, the powerful *Oregon* leading, with the *Brooklyn* and *Texas* not far behind. The rain of steel continued, and at last, burning like her sister ships, the *Vizcaya* turned shoreward, and many of her crew leaped overboard to save their lives.

Only the *Colon* now remained. She was still in fair condition, and it was the Spaniards' ardent hope to save at least one ship from the dire calamity that had overtaken them. But this was not to be, and after a run of a few miles, during which the *Oregon* and *Brooklyn* continued to pound her with shot and shell, the Spanish flag was lowered, and the *Colon* also ran ashore.

It was assuredly a mighty victory, a fitting mate to the great victory won by Admiral Dewey, and when the news reached our country there was such a Fourth of July celebration everywhere as will never be forgotten. Twice had our navy met the ships of Spain, and each time we had sunk every vessel without losing any of our own. More than this, while the Spaniards had lost many men through shot and fire and drowning, our total loss was but one man killed and a handful wounded.

The loss of her second fleet was a bitter blow to Spain, and many predicted that the war would not continue much longer, and this prediction proved correct.

During the rush made by the Rough Riders and our other soldiers, they had gone right through several bodies of Spanish guerillas who were secreted in the trees of the jungle. These guerillas, really lawless fellows belonging to no particular command, could not get back into Santiago because of the strong American guard at the intrenchments, and consequently they contented themselves with remaining out of sight and peppering our soldiers whenever the opportunity offered.

"This will not do," said Theodore Roosevelt. "They are shooting down our men without giving them a chance to fire back. We'll have to get after them." And without delay he sent out a detachment of the best Rough Rider shots to be found. These sharpshooters searched the jungle back of the intrenchments thoroughly, and as a result killed eleven of the guerillas and wounded many more. After that the guerillas kept their distance, satisfied that the Yankees could beat them at their own game.

CHAPTER XVII

DEVOTION OF THE ROUGH RIDERS TO THEODORE ROOSEVELT HIS KINDNESS TO HIS MEN LAST OF THE FIGHTING THE TRUCE AND TREATY OF PEACE

With the defeat of Admiral Cervera's fleet, a flag of truce was sent into Santiago by the commander of our army, demanding the surrender of the city. While these negotiations were pending, all fighting came to an end, and the Rough Riders had but little to do outside of making themselves comfortable and caring for the many who were getting sick because of the lack of shelter and proper food. Food was now coming in more rapidly, and soon all were supplied with tents and blankets. During this time Theodore Roosevelt's personal baggage appeared, and he celebrated the arrival by treating himself to a shave and a change of linen, something impossible to do since the fighting had begun.

In his own writings, Mr. Roosevelt has spoken at great length of the devotion which all of the Rough Riders displayed toward him. They were anxious to wait on him at all hours of the day and night. Some would pitch his tent, others would clean his weapons, and still others would go hunting and bring in such game as the vicinity afforded. When ordered to do anything, there was rarely a grumble. Those in the hospital bore their sufferings with remarkable fortitude.

In return for this, Theodore Roosevelt did all he could to make life less hard for those under him. The game that was brought to him he sent to the hospital, that the wounded might have proper nourishment; and he either went himself or sent somebody to the seacoast, to purchase food which the commissary department possessed, but which, through lack of organization, it was slow in distributing. When no shelter was to be had, he slept on the ground with his men, and when they had to work on the trenches at night, he was up and around superintending the labor.

"He was one of us, and he let us know it," was said by one of the Rough Riders. "He ate the same food we did, and he was mighty good to the sick and the wounded. He paid for lots of things out of his own pocket, and I don't believe he has ever asked Uncle Sam to pay him back."

There was no telling how soon the truce would come to an end and fighting would begin again, and night after night the Rough Riders were kept on guard. There was a standing order that each fourth man should keep awake while the others slept, and no matter how dark or rainy the night, Theodore Roosevelt tramped around from one trench to another, seeing to it that this order was obeyed. He also visited the intrenchments of other commands, to compare them and make certain that the grade of service was equally high among the Rough Riders. This shows distinctly that he was a natural-born military commander.

The truce lasted a week, and while all operations were supposed to have come to an end, both the Americans and the Spaniards spent the time in strengthening their positions. At one time the Americans constructed a fairly good defence, in which they placed two Gatling guns and two automatic Colt guns, and this was named Fort Roosevelt, in honor of the Rough Rider commander.

On the tenth of July the fighting began once more, and again the batteries on both sides sent shot and shell into the camps of the enemy. It was largely fighting at long range, and the only Rough Riders who took part were those who manned the Colt's guns, and a small body of sharpshooters stationed in a trench well to the front.

On the next day the Rough Riders were ordered northward, to guard the road running from Santiago to El Caney. Here some fighting was in progress, and the troopers expected to get into battle once more. But the skirmish came to an end before they arrived, very much to their disappointment.

Hardly had the Rough Riders settled in their new position than a storm came up which proved to be the heaviest yet experienced during the campaign. While Theodore Roosevelt was sleeping in his tent, the shelter was blown down and away, and all of his personal effects were scattered in the mud and wet. As best he could, he donned his clothing, saw to it that his men were safe, and then betook himself to a kitchen tent, where he finished the sleep of that night on a rude table recently taken from an abandoned Spanish home in that vicinity.

"On that night it rained cats and dogs and hammer-handles," said one of the soldiers afterward. "It was inky dark darker than I have ever known it to be anywhere on the plains. The water made a muddy pond of the whole camp, and the trenches were half filled in no time. Everything was blown helter-skelter by the furious wind, and some of our outfits we never recovered. In the midst of the confusion some fellows reported that the Spaniards were trying to break through our lines, but the report was false, the outsiders were starving Cubans who had come in looking for shelter and something to eat. We gave them what we could which was precious little, for we had next to nothing ourselves and then got them to help us get things together again. One of the Cubans was an old man, who could speak a little English. He said he had lost two daughters and three grandchildren by starvation since the war between Spain and Cuba had started. He himself was little more than a skeleton."

That Theodore Roosevelt was warmhearted enough to look out for other soldiers besides those of his own command is proven by what took place on the day following the big storm. Next to the Rough Riders were located a regiment of Illinois Volunteers. Because of the muddy roads and swollen streams, they could get no rations, and scant as were their own supplies, Colonel Roosevelt had the Rough Riders furnish them with beans, coffee, and a few cases of hardtack, for which they were extremely grateful. Later in the day the commander of the Rough Riders also got to them part of a mule train of provisions.

The American position had been greatly strengthened, and many additional troops were now at the front. It was felt that an advance upon Santiago would surely result in victory, although the losses might be large. But the Spaniards were no longer in a position to continue the struggle, and on July 17 the city formally surrendered. The surrendered territory covered many miles, and the Spanish soldiers to lay down their arms numbered upward of twenty thousand.

There was great cheering in the American trenches when the glad news was brought in, and soon Old Glory was planted on every height, while the trumpets sounded out triumphantly. Possession of Santiago was immediate, and in a few hours the Stars and Stripes floated from the flagstaff of the civil government buildings. Our gallant army had won on the land just as our gallant navy had won on the sea. The war had been, for us, one of triumph from start to finish.

In foreign countries the news was received with an astonishment that can scarcely be described. After Dewey's wonderful victory in Manila Bay, many naval experts said that such a fight could not be duplicated, yet it was duplicated two months later off Santiago Bay in a manner that left no doubt of American supremacy on the sea. Then when it came to fighting on land, our army was designated as "paper" soldiers, that is, soldiers on paper or in name only, and it was said that their guns would be found of little use against the Mausers of Spain. But this was likewise false; and to-day the army and navy of the United States are respected everywhere. And more than this, foreign powers have come to our country for many of their war-ships, asking us to build and equip them, and also asking us to make cannon and rifles for them.

While the war was on in Cuba, a part of the United States army under General Miles was sent to Porto Rico, another island belonging to Spain. Here the inhabitants hailed the Americans with delight, and the resistance by the Spanish soldiers was only half-hearted.

With the downfall of the navy and Santiago, Spain knew not what to do next, and gladly received the terms of peace offered by President McKinley and his advisers. The terms were accepted on August 9, and thus the short but sharp war came to a termination. By the treaty of peace Cuba was given her liberty, and Porto Rico and the Philippines passed into the possession of the United States.

CHAPTER XVIII

LAST DAYS IN CUBA THE DEPARTURE FOR HOME ARRIVAL AT MONTAUK CARING FOR THE SICK AND WOUNDED PRESENTATION TO THEODORE ROOSEVELT BY HIS MEN MUSTERING-OUT OF THE ROUGH RIDERS

Four days after the surrender of Santiago the Rough Riders found themselves in the hills four or five miles back from the intrenchments they had occupied during the last fight. Other commands were scattered in various directions, for to let them go into the wretched city would have been out of the question. Santiago was dirty in the extreme; the fever was there, and hundreds were on the verge of starvation.

It was a trying time for everybody, and equally so for Theodore Roosevelt, who did all in his power, as before, to make his men comfortable. When it did not rain, the sun came out fiercely, causing a rapid evaporation that was thoroughly exhausting to the soldiers. The locality was not a healthy one, and soon scores of Rough Riders and others were down with malaria or fever. Doctors and surgeons were scarce, and hospital accommodations were scanty, and again and again did Colonel Roosevelt send down on his own account to the seacoast and to Santiago for food and medicines of which his command were in dire need. He was now colonel of the Rough Riders in reality, his promotion having been granted to him just one week after the heroic charge up San Juan Hill. His old colonel, Wood, was installed at Santiago as military governor. This, for the time being, left Colonel Roosevelt in command of the cavalry brigade, no small honor to one who had been, but a few months before, a stranger to military duties.

During this time in camp, Theodore Roosevelt visited Santiago and the forts at the entrance to the harbor, and with the pen of a skilled author he has, in one of his books, given us vivid pictures of the sights to be seen there at that time the crooked streets with their queer shops, the wretched inhabitants, the grim and frowning forts, all hemmed in by the towering mountains and the sea. He likewise tells of his trips to the mountains, and how his companions were usually exhausted by the climbing done. For one who in his youth had been so delicate, he stood the exposure remarkably well, for which he was thankful.

For some time the authorities at Washington did not know what to do with the troops in Cuba. It was suggested that they move up to higher ground, or to another neighborhood. But General Shafter knew, and so did all of the officers under him, that to keep the army in the island would only mean more sickness and death.

"I will go to the general with a protest," said Colonel Roosevelt. And he did so. Meanwhile the other head officers drew up a letter of protest, and this was signed by all, including the commander of the Rough Riders. In his own letter Roosevelt protested against the treatment of his men in the matter of rations, clothing, and hospital accommodations, and in the other letter, called by the officers a Round Robin, there was a protest about remaining in Cuba longer, with the fever getting worse every day. These letters were made public through the press of the United States, with the result that the troops were ordered home without further delay.

The Rough Riders left Cuba on August 7, just six weeks and a half after landing. The time spent in the island had been short, but to many it seemed an age. None were sorry to depart, although sad to think that some of the sick had to be left behind.

The transport used this time was the *Miami*, and Mr. Roosevelt tells us that, taken as a whole, the accommodations were better than they had been on the *Yucatan*. But on the trip much trouble was had with some of the stokers and engineers, who insisted upon drinking some liquor smuggled aboard.

"I will not permit this," said Colonel Roosevelt. And he read the disorderly ones a strong lecture and made them give up their liquor. After that, as there was much grumbling, he set a guard; and that was the end of that trouble.

The destination of the transport was Montauk, on the extreme eastern shore of Long Island. The trip took nine days, rather a dreary time to those anxious to see their native land once more. When an anchorage was gained, a gunboat came out to the transport with the welcome news that Spain had agreed to our terms.

The sick had still to be cared for; yet, taken as a whole, the month spent at the camp at Montauk was pleasant enough. Here Colonel Roosevelt met that part of the regiment that had been left behind in Florida, and all the stories of the fights had to be told over and over again.

"It was good to meet the rest of the regiment," says Mr. Roosevelt, in his book. "They all felt dreadfully at not having been in Cuba. Of course those who stayed had done their duty precisely as did those who went." Which was true; yet, as he adds, those who had been left behind could not be comforted.

Colonel Roosevelt was still in charge of the brigade while at Montauk, and much of his time was taken up in getting out necessary reports, and seeing to it that the entire camp was kept in first-class sanitary condition.

"And he was up to the mark," said one of those who were there. "He didn't allow the least bit of dirt, and everything had to be as shipshape as if we were at West Point. And it was a good thing, too, for it kept the sickness from spreading."

The sea-breeze is strong at Montauk, and this soon began to tell upon all who were sick, putting in them new life and vigor. Here every possible attention was given to those who were down, so that ere long many were up again and as well as ever.

When he had a little time to himself, Theodore Roosevelt would gather a few friends around him, and either go to the beach to bathe or go off on a long horseback ride. War was to him a thing of the past, and he was once more willing to become a private citizen as of old.

In those days the camp at Montauk was constantly crowded with visitors from New York City and elsewhere, who poured in upon every train. All of the soldiers who had been to Cuba were hailed as heroes, and had to tell their stories many times.

"Every soldier had a crowd following him," said one private. "The visitors wanted to know how we had fought, how we had been treated by the government, how things looked in Cuba, and a hundred and one other things. Most of the visitors, especially the ladies, wanted our autographs, and I had to write mine as many as forty times a day. I remember one of the men, a cowboy from Oklahoma, couldn't write, and he got so upset over this that every time somebody asked him for his autograph he would run away, saying he had forgotten to do something that he had been ordered to do. When I and some chums went down to New York to look around, all the folks stared at us, and many insisted on shaking hands and treating."

COLONEL ROOSEVELT AT MONTAUK POINT.
(Photograph by Pach Bros., New York.)

The uniforms the Rough Riders had worn in Cuba were in rags, and many had boarded the transport barefooted. The rags were saved as trophies of the occasion, and many are still in existence.

At Camp Wykoff, as the place was called, there was a large hospital for the sick, and to this many came to do what they could for the sufferers, who were now given every possible attention. Among the visitors was Miss Helen Gould, who had used her ample means for the benefit of the sick all through the war, and who now continued to play the good Samaritan. President McKinley and many of his cabinet likewise visited the camp, and saw to it that everything in the hospital and out of it was as it should be. The sick were presented with the best of fruits and other things, and many ladies assisted the nurses by reading to the patients and by writing letters for them.

Now that they had nothing to do in the shape of fighting, many of the Rough Riders were anxious to get back to the wild West. Life in an ordinary camp did not suit them, and at every available opportunity they indulged in "horse play," working off many practical jokes upon each other.

One day a report went the rounds that a member of another cavalry organization could not master a certain horse that had been assigned to him. The report was true, for the horse was what is called by ranchmen a "bad bucker."

"I think Sergeant Darnell can master him," said Colonel Roosevelt.

He referred to one of the best "bronco busters" among the Rough Riders, a man who had never yet allowed a steed to get the best of him.

"All right, let Darnell try him," said others. And a test was arranged for the day following.

At that time Secretary of War Alger was in camp, and a great crowd of visitors, military men and others, gathered before Colonel Roosevelt's quarters to watch the contest. At the proper time the vicious horse was brought forth, and watching his chance, Sergeant Darnell leaped upon his back. Then came such a bucking, leaping, and prancing as many had never witnessed before.

"He'll be killed!" cried many of the ladies. "The horse will have him under in another moment." But such fears were groundless. Darnell knew exactly what he was doing, and in the end the fiery steed had to give in, completely conquered.

On the last Sunday in camp, Chaplain Brown delivered an impressive sermon, to which all listened with grave attention. After he had finished, Theodore Roosevelt spoke to the men in a feeling way.

"I told them how proud I was of them," he says. "But warned them not to think that they could go back and rest on their laurels, bidding them remember that though for ten days or so the world would be willing to treat them as heroes, yet after that time they would find they would have to get down to hard work just like anybody else, unless they were willing to be regarded as worthless do-nothings." This was the best possible advice, and it is believed that many of the soldiers profited by it.

Before the men were mustered out, they treated their beloved commander to a genuine surprise. They had had a fine bronze of a "Bronco Buster" made, and this was presented to Colonel Roosevelt on behalf of the whole regiment. It touched him deeply, and to-day this bronze is one of his most highly prized gifts.

At last came news that the Rough Riders would be mustered out of the United States service the next day. That evening a great celebration took place, in which all of the men joined, each according to his own notion of what a celebration should be. Large bonfires were lit, and here some delivered speeches, the soldiers from the colleges sang, those with Indian blood in them gave a characteristic dance, and cowboys and ranchmen did "double-shuffles" and "cut up" as suited them.

On the morning of September 15, four months after the Rough Riders had been organized, the colors were lowered in camp, the men were mustered out, and officers and privates shook hands and said good-by.

"It was the greatest sight I ever saw," says one of the number. "Not until that moment came did we realize what it meant to part with those who had fought with us in battle and suffered the hardships of life in the trenches. Strange friendships had been formed, some between those who were very rich and very poor, and others between those who were well educated and very ignorant. One man who was studying for a professional life had as his particular chum a rough cowboy who had never spent six months over his books. But the two had stood by each other and suffered, and I really believe they were willing to lay down their lives for each other.

"Many of the men could hardly bear to part with Colonel Roosevelt. He had stuck by them through thick and thin, and they worshipped him. Some shook hands half a dozen times, and some hardly dared to speak for fear of breaking down. I never expect to see the match of that scene again."

CHAPTER XIX

Nominated for Governor of New York A Rough Rider Way of Campaigning Elected Governor Important Work at Albany The Homestead at Oyster Bay Chopping down a Tree for Exercise

The war with Spain was at an end, and Uncle Sam had now to turn his attention to the Philippines, where for many months to come military disturbances of a more or less serious nature were to take place.

Theodore Roosevelt might have remained in the army, and had he done so there is no doubt but that he would have swiftly risen to a rank of importance.

But the people of the State of New York willed otherwise.

"He is a great military man," they said. "But he was likewise a fine Police Commissioner and a Civil Service Commissioner, fighting continually for what was right and good. Let us make him our next governor."

The convention that nominated Theodore Roosevelt for the highest office in the Empire State met at Saratoga, September 27, 1898, just twelve days after the Rough Riders were mustered out. At that time Frank S. Black was governor of the state, having been elected two years before by a large majority. The governor had many friends, and they said he deserved another term.

"Roosevelt is not a citizen of this state," said they. "He gave up his residence here when he went to Washington to become Assistant Secretary of the Navy."

"We don't want him anyway," said other politicians, who had not forgotten how the Rough Rider had acted when in the Assembly. "If he gets into office, it will be impossible to manage him." And they worked night and day to defeat the hero of San Juan Hill.

On the day of the convention, the hall where it was held was jammed with people. The people were also crowded in the street outside, and on every hand were seen Rough Rider badges.

"It was a Roosevelt crowd from top to bottom," says one who was there. "You heard his name everywhere in the hotels, on the streets, no matter where you went. Every once in a while somebody would shout, 'Three cheers for Teddy!' and the cheers would be given with a will."

As soon as the convention had settled down to business, Governor Black was put up for nomination, and then the Hon. Chauncey M. Depew presented the name of Theodore Roosevelt. He spoke of what had been done in Cuba, and added:

"The Rough Riders endured no hardships nor dangers which were not shared by their Colonel. He helped them dig their ditches; he stood beside them in the deadly dampness of the trenches. No floored tent for him if his comrades must sleep on the ground and under the sky. In that world-famed charge of the Rough Riders up the hill of San Juan, their Colonel was a hundred feet in advance."

There was a prolonged cheering when Theodore Roosevelt's name was mentioned, and hundreds waved their handkerchiefs and flags. Other speeches followed, and at last came the voting. Out of the total number cast Theodore Roosevelt received seven hundred and fifty-three and Governor Black two hundred and eighteen.

"I move we make the nomination of Theodore Roosevelt unanimous!" cried Judge Cady, who had previously presented the name of Governor Black. And amid continued cheering this was done.

Theodore Roosevelt had been nominated on the regular Republican ticket. In opposition, the Democrats nominated Augustus Van Wyck, also well known, and likewise of as old Dutch stock as Roosevelt himself.

The campaign was a decidedly strenuous one. The Democrats made every effort to win, while on the other hand the Republicans who had wanted Governor Black for another term did not give to Mr. Roosevelt the support promised when his nomination had been made unanimous.

"We shall be defeated," said more than one friend to Roosevelt. "It seems a shame, but we cannot arouse the party as it should be aroused."

"I will see what I can do myself," answered the former leader of the Rough Riders. And he arranged to make a complete tour of the State, taking in almost every city and town of importance. When some of the old campaign managers heard of this, they came to Roosevelt in great alarm.

"You mustn't do it," they said. "It will ruin you."

"I will risk it," was the answer of the candidate. And forthwith he started on his tour, taking a handful of his Rough Rider friends with him.

It was a brilliant stroke on the part of Theodore Roosevelt, and it told tremendously in his favor. Wherever he went, the people turned out in large crowds to see him and to listen to what he or his Rough Rider companions had to say. Citizens by the hundred came up to shake him by the hand and wish him success. Parades were organized to do him honor, and at night there would be brilliant illuminations and fireworks.

"We have aroused the party," said he, when the tour was at an end. And so it proved. Although Van Wyck was popular, Theodore Roosevelt was elected to the high office of governor by seventeen thousand plurality.

It was certainly a high position for such a young man to occupy. He was barely forty years of age, yet as governor of New York he ruled twice as many people as did George Washington when first President of the United States.

He entered on his new duties with as much zeal as he had displayed when organizing the Rough Riders, and in a few weeks had the reins of government well in hand. It is said that while he was governor he was never surprised by those who opposed him. When they wanted facts and figures he was able to produce them, and he never supported or vetoed a measure unless he was morally certain he was on the right side. He was open-faced to the last degree, and what he said he meant.

During his term of office many measures of importance were considered, but in a work of this kind it is not necessary to go into details. For several important offices he nominated men of his own selection, despite the protests of some older politicians, and these selections proved first-class.

During his term as governor, Mr. Roosevelt did a great work for many poor people in New York City, who worked in what are called "sweat shops," small, close quarters, not fit for working purposes, in which men, women, and children make clothing and other articles. He enforced what was known as the Factory Law, and the owners of the "sweat-shops" had to seek larger and more sanitary quarters for their employees. He also took a strong hand in reforming the administration of the canals, which had been one-sided and unfair.

But perhaps his greatest work was in behalf of a measure meant to make the great corporations of New York State pay their fair share of the general taxes. In the past these corporations had had great rights conferred upon them, and they had paid little or nothing in return.

"This is unjust," said Governor Roosevelt. "They should pay their taxes just as the poorest citizen is compelled to pay his tax."

When the corporations heard this, many of the men in control were furious, and they threatened the governor in all sorts of ways. They would defeat him if he ever again came up for election, and defeat him so badly that he would never again be heard of.

"Do as you please, gentlemen," said the governor. "I am here to do my duty, and I intend to do it." And he called an extra session of the legislature for that purpose. It is said that much money was used by some corporations to defeat Governor Roosevelt's will, but in the end a modified form of the bill was passed. Since that time other bills along similar lines have become laws; so that the great corporations have to pay millions of dollars which in the past they had escaped paying. Such measures are of immense benefit to the ordinary citizen, and for his share in this work Theodore Roosevelt deserves great credit.

It was while governor of New York that Mr. Roosevelt gave to the public his book entitled "The Rough Riders." It contains a history of that organization from his personal point of view, and makes the most fascinating kind of reading from beginning to end. It was well received, and added not a little to the laurels of the writer as an author.

Although much of his time was spent at Albany as Executive, Theodore Roosevelt had not given up the old homestead at Oyster Bay on Long Island, and thither he went for rest and recreation, taking his entire family, which, as has been said, consisted of his wife and six children, with him.

The old Roosevelt homestead is on a hill about three miles distant from the village. The road to the house winds upward through a wilderness of trees and brushwood. At the top of the hill, where the house stands, is a cleared space, free to the strong breezes of Long Island Sound. It is on the north shore, about twenty-five miles from City Hall, New York.

The house is a large, three-story affair, with crossed gables, and a large semicircular veranda at one end. Inside there is a wide hall, and all the rooms are of good size, with broad windows and inviting open fireplaces. One room is fitted up as Mr. Roosevelt's "den," with many bookcases filled with books, and with rare prints of Washington, Lincoln, and other celebrities on the walls, and with not a few trophies of the hunt added. In this room Mr. Roosevelt has done much of his work as an author.

It is said that Abraham Lincoln not only chopped wood for a living, but that he rather enjoyed the outdoor exercise. Be that as it may, it remains a fact that Mr. Roosevelt frequently goes forth into the woods on his estate to fell a tree, or split one up, just for the exercise thus afforded. This he did while he was governor of New York, and once astonished some newspaper men who had come to see him on business by the dexterity with which he cut a large tree trunk in two. He even invited his visitors to "take a hack at it" themselves, but they respectfully declined.

He still kept up his athletic exercise, and one of his favorite amusements was to go on long horseback rides, either alone, or with some relative or friend. At other times he would go deep into the woods with his young sons, showing them how to bring down the nuts from the trees, or how to use their guns on any small game that chanced to show itself. His family life was then, as it has always been, a happy one; but of this let us speak later.

THE ROOSEVELT HOMESTEAD AT OYSTER BAY.
(*Photograph by Pach Bros., N.Y.*)]

CHAPTER XX

GREAT RECEPTION TO ADMIRAL DEWEY GOVERNOR ROOSEVELT'S INCREASED POPULARITY LAST ANNUAL MESSAGE AS GOVERNOR VISIT TO CHICAGO REMARKABLE SPEECH ON THE STRENUOUS LIFE

Although the war with Spain was over, the people of the United States had not forgotten the wonderful work accomplished by Admiral Dewey and his men at Manila, and when the dauntless naval fighter returned to this country, people everywhere arose to do him honor.

"He well deserves it," said Governor Roosevelt. And he appointed September 29 and 30, 1899, as public holidays, to be observed throughout the entire State as days of general thanksgiving. These days were commonly called "Dewey Days."

The reception to the Admiral and to the other naval heroes was to take place in New York and vicinity, and for many days the citizens were busy decorating their homes and places of business with flags and bunting and pictures, and immense signs of "Welcome," some in letters several feet long. At the junction of Broadway, Fifth Avenue, and Twenty-Third Street, an immense triumphal arch was erected, and reviewing stands stretched along the line of parade for many miles.

On the day before the grand reception, Governor Roosevelt, with some members of his staff, called upon Admiral Dewey on board of the *Olympia*, and offered the State's greeting. A pleasant time was had by all, and the governor assured the sea hero that the people of New York and vicinity were more than anxious to do him honor.

It had been arranged that a naval parade should be held on the first day of the reception, and a land parade on the day following. The course of the naval parade was up the Hudson River past Grant's Tomb, and the grand procession on the water included the *Olympia*, the Admiral's flag-ship, and the *New York, Indiana, Massachusetts, Texas, Brooklyn*, and a large number of other war-ships of lesser importance, besides an immense number of private steam-yachts and other craft.

The day dawned clear and bright, and the banks of the Hudson were lined from end to end with people. When the procession of war-ships swept up the stream, loud was the applause, while flags waved everywhere, and whistles blew constantly. When passing Grant's Tomb every war-ship fired a salute, and the mass of sound echoing across the water was positively deafening.

As the *Olympia* swept up the river, fired her salute, and then came to anchor a short distance below the last resting-place of General Grant, Admiral Dewey stood on the bridge of his flag-ship, a small, trim figure, with a smile and a wave of the hand for everybody. The surging people could see him but indistinctly, yet there was much hand clapping, and throats grew sore with cheering.

But there was another figure in that naval parade, the person of one also dear to the hearts of the people. It was the figure of Theodore Roosevelt, dressed, not as a Rough Rider, but as a civilian, standing at the rail of a steamer used by the New York State officials. When the people saw and recognized that figure, the cheering was as wild as ever.

"It is Roosevelt!" ran from mouth to mouth. "The hero of San Juan Hill!"

"Hurrah for the Rough Riders and their gallant leader!" came from others. And the cheering was renewed.

In the evening there was a grand display of fireworks and illuminated floats. The immense span of the Brooklyn Bridge was a mass of lights, and contained the words "Welcome, Dewey" in lettering which covered several hundred feet. All of the war-ships had their search-lights in operation, and it can truthfully be said that for once the metropolis was as light as day.

But all of this was as nothing compared with the land parade which followed. Never before had the streets of New York been so jammed with people. At many points it was impossible to move, yet the crowds were good-natured and patriotic to the core. The parade started at Grant's Tomb and ended at Washington Square, and was between five and six hours in passing. Admiral Dewey rode in a carriage with Mayor Van Wyck, and received another ovation. At the Triumphal Arch the Admiral reviewed the parade, and here he was accorded additional honors.

In this parade Governor Roosevelt rode on horseback, in civilian dress. As he came down the street, the immense crowds recognized him from afar, and the hand clapping and cheering was tremendous, and lasted long after he was out of sight.

"It's our own Teddy Roosevelt!" cried the more enthusiastic.

"Hurrah for the governor! Hurrah for the colonel of the Rough Riders!"

"Hurrah for the coming President!" said another. And he spoke better than he knew.

This demonstration came straight from the people's heart, and it could not help but affect Theodore Roosevelt. Sitting astride of his dark-colored horse like a veteran, he bowed right and left. Next to Dewey, he was easily the greatest figure in the parade.

On January 3, 1900, Governor Roosevelt sent his last annual message to the State legislature. It was an able document, and as it was now recognized everywhere that he was a truly national figure, it was given careful attention. It treated of the corruption in canal management, of the franchise tax, of taxation in general, and a large portion was devoted to the trusts. At that time the trusts were receiving great attention everywhere, and it was felt that what the governor had to say about them, that they were largely over-capitalized, that they misrepresented the condition of their affairs, that they promoted unfair competition, and that they wielded increased power over the wage-earner, was strictly true.

In Chicago there is a wealthy organization known as the Hamilton Club, and the members were very anxious to have Governor Roosevelt as their guest on Appomattox Day, April 10, 1899. A delegation went to New York to invite the governor, and he accepted the invitation with pleasure.

"The middle West is very dear to me," said he. "It will be a pleasure to meet my many friends there."

Of course he was expected to speak, and said the subject of his address would be "The Strenuous Life," certainly a subject close to his own heart, considering the life he himself had led.

When Mr. Roosevelt reached the metropolis of the Great Lakes, he found a large crowd waiting at the railroad station to receive him. The reception committee was on hand, with the necessary coaches, and people were crowded everywhere, anxious to catch a sight of the man who had made himself famous by the advance up San Juan Hill.

But for the moment Governor Roosevelt did not see the reception committee, nor did he see the great mass of people. In a far corner of the platform he caught sight of six men, dressed in the faded and tattered uniform of the Rough Riders. They were not men of wealth or position, but they were men of his old command, and he had not forgotten them.

"Glad to see you, boys, glad to see you!" he shouted, as he elbowed his way toward them. "Come up here and shake hands."

"Glad to see you, Colonel," was the ready answer, and the faces of the men broke into broad smiles. They shook hands readily, and willingly answered all of the questions the governor put to them. He asked how each of them was doing, calling them by their names, and concluded by requesting them to come up to the Auditorium later, "for an all-round chat."

"It was a great meeting," said one who was there. "Before the train came in, those old Rough Riders were nervous and showed it. They knew that Roosevelt had become a great man, and they were just a little afraid he would pass them by. When the meeting was over, they went off as happy as a lot of children, and one of them said, 'Say, fellows, Teddy's just all right yet, ain't he?' And another answered: 'Told you he would be. He's a white man through and through, none whiter anywhere.'"

The banquet was held in the Auditorium Theatre building, and was said to be the largest ever given in Chicago. Many distinguished guests were present, both from the North and the South, and the place was a mass of flowers and brilliantly illuminated, while a fine orchestra discoursed music during the meal. When Theodore Roosevelt arose to speak, there was cheering that lasted fully a quarter of an hour.

The speech made upon this occasion is one not likely to be forgotten. Previous to that time the word "strenuous" had been heard but seldom, but ever since it has stood for something definite, and is much in use. In part Mr. Roosevelt spoke as follows:

"I wish to preach, not the doctrine of ignoble ease, but the doctrine of the strenuous life; the life of toil and effort; of labor and strife; to preach that highest form of success which comes, not to the man who desires mere easy peace, but to the man who does not shirk from danger, from hardship, or from bitter toil, and who out of these wins the splendid ultimate triumph."

Another paragraph is equally interesting and elevating:

"We do not admire the man of timid peace. We admire the man who embodies victorious effort; the man who never wrongs his neighbor, who is prompt to help a friend; but who has those virile qualities necessary to win in the stern strife of actual life. It is hard to fail; but it is worse never to have tried to succeed."

And to this he adds:

"As it is with the individual so it is with the nation. It is a base untruth to say that happy is the nation that has no history. Thrice happy is the nation that has a glorious history. Far better is it to dare mighty things to win glorious triumphs, even though checkered by failure, than to take rank with those poor spirits who neither enjoy much nor suffer much, because they live in the gray twilight that knows neither victory nor defeat."[1]

Theodore Roosevelt

CHAPTER XXI

THE CONVENTION AT PHILADELPHIA THEODORE ROOSEVELT SECONDS THE NOMINATION OF PRESIDENT MCKINLEY BECOMES CANDIDATE FOR THE VICE-PRESIDENCY REMARKABLE TOURS THROUGH MANY STATES

As the time came on to nominate parties for the office of President and Vice-President of the United States, in 1900, there was considerable speculation in the Republican party regarding who should be chosen for the second name on the ticket.

It was felt by everybody that President McKinley had honestly earned a second term, not alone by his management of the war with Spain, but also because of his stand touching the rebellion in the Philippines, and on other matters of equal importance.

About the Vice-Presidency the political managers were not so sure, and they mentioned several names. But in the hearts of the people there was but one name, and that was Theodore Roosevelt.

"We must have him," was heard upon every side. "He will be just the right man in the right place. He will give to the office an importance never before attached to it, and an importance which it deserves."

Personally, Governor Roosevelt did not wish this added honor. As the Executive of the greatest State in our Union, he had started great reforms, and he wanted to finish them.

"My work is here," he said to many. "Let me do what I have been called to do, and then I will again be at the service of the whole nation once more."

The National Republican Convention met in Philadelphia, June 19, in Exposition Hall, beautifully decorated with flags and banners. Senator Mark Hanna, President McKinley's warmest personal friend, was chairman, and the delegates, numbering over seven hundred, came, as usual at such conventions, from every State in the Union. Governor Roosevelt himself was a delegate, and sat near the middle aisle, five or six seats from the front. He was recognized by everybody, and it is safe to say that he was the most conspicuous figure at the convention.

Up to the last minute many of the political leaders were, in a measure, afraid of Theodore Roosevelt. They understood his immense popularity, and were afraid that the convention might be "stampeded" in his favor.

"If they once start to yell for Roosevelt, it will be good-by to everybody else," said one old politician. "They are just crazy after the leader of the Rough Riders."

But this man did not understand the stern moral honesty of the man under consideration. Roosevelt believed in upholding William McKinley, and had said so, and it was no more possible for him to seek the Presidential nomination by an underhanded trick than it was for President McKinley to do an equally base thing when he was asked to allow his name to be mentioned at the time he had pledged himself to support John Sherman.[2] Both men were of equal loyalty, and the word of each was as good as his bond.

It was Senator Foraker who put up President McKinley for nomination, and the vigorous cheering at that time will never be forgotten. Fifteen thousand throats yelled themselves hoarse, and then broke into the ringing words and music of "The Union Forever!" in a manner that made the very convention hall tremble. Then came cries for Roosevelt, "For our own Teddy of the Rough Riders!" and, written speech in hand, he arose amid that vast multitude to second the candidacy of William McKinley. Not once did he look at the paper he held in his hand, but with a force that could not be misunderstood he addressed the assemblage.

"I rise to second the nomination of William McKinley, because with him as a leader this people has trod the path of national greatness and prosperity with the strides of a giant," said he, "and because under him we can and will succeed in the election. Exactly as in the past we have remedied the evils which we undertook to remedy, so now when we say that a wrong shall be righted, it most assuredly will be righted.

"We stand on the threshold of a new century, a century big with the fate of the great nations of the earth. It rests with us to decide now whether in the opening years of that century we shall march forward to fresh triumphs, or whether at the outset we shall deliberately cripple ourselves for the contest."

His speech was the signal for another burst of applause, and when finally Theodore Roosevelt was named as the candidate for Vice-President, the crowd yelled until it could yell no longer, while many sang "Yankee Doodle" and other more or less patriotic airs, keeping time with canes and flag-sticks. When the vote was cast, only one delegate failed to vote for Theodore Roosevelt, and that was Theodore Roosevelt himself.

The platform of the party was largely a repetition of the platform of four years before. Again the cry was for "sound money," and for the continuance of President McKinley's policy in the Philippines.

The campaign which followed was truly a strenuous one to use a favorite word of the candidate. President McKinley decided not to make many speeches, and thus the hard work previous to election day fell upon Theodore Roosevelt.

He did not shirk the task. As with everything he undertook, he entered into the campaign with vigor, resolved to deserve success even if he did not win it.

"I will do my best in the interests of our party, and for the benefit of the people at large," said Theodore Roosevelt. "No man can do more than that."

In the few short months between the time when he was nominated and when the election was held, Governor Roosevelt travelled over 20,000 miles by rail, visiting nearly 600 towns, and addressing, on a rough estimate, fully 3,000,000 of people! In that time he delivered 673 speeches, some of them half an hour and some an hour in length.

In his thousands of miles of travel the candidate for the Vice-Presidency visited many States, particularly those lying between New York and Colorado. At nearly every town he was greeted by an immense crowd, all anxious to do the leader of the Rough Riders honor. In the large cities great banquets were held, and he was shown much respect and consideration. In many places those who had fought under him came to see and listen to him, and these meetings were of especial pleasure. Often he would see an old Rough Rider hanging back in the crowd, and would call him to the front or do his best to reach the ex-soldier and shake him by the hand.

One occurrence is worthy of special mention. The Democratic party had nominated William Jennings Bryan as their candidate for President. There was a great labor picnic and demonstration at Chicago, and both Governor Roosevelt and Mr. Bryan were invited to speak.

"You had better not accept, governor," said some friends to Theodore Roosevelt. "There may be trouble."

"I am not afraid," answered the former leader of the Rough Riders.

"But Mr. Bryan and yourself are to be there at practically the same time."

"That does not matter," said the governor. And he went to Chicago on September 3, to attend the Labor Day celebrations. The picnic was held at Electric Park, and in the presence of fifteen thousand people Governor Roosevelt and Mr. Bryan "buried the hatchet" for the time being, and spoke to those surrounding them on the dignity of labor and the duties of the laboring man to better himself and his social conditions. In that motley collection of people there were frequent cries of "Hurrah for Teddy!" and "What's the matter with Bryan? He's all right!" but there was no disturbance, and each speaker was listened to with respectful attention from start to finish. It was without a doubt a meeting to show true American liberty and free speech at its best.

But all of the stops on his tours were not so pleasant to Governor Roosevelt. In every community there are those who are low-bred and bound to make an exhibition of their baseness. At Waverly, New York, a stone was flung at him through the car window, breaking the glass but missing the candidate for whom it was intended. At once there was excitement.

"Are you hurt, Governor?" was the question asked.

"No," returned Theodore Roosevelt. And then he added, with a faint smile, "It's only a bouquet, but I wish, after this, they wouldn't make them quite so hard."

There was also a demonstration against the candidate at Haverstraw, New York, which threatened for a while to break up an intended meeting. But the worst rowdyism was encountered at Victor, a small town in Colorado, near the well-known mining centre of Cripple Creek. Victor was full of miners who wanted not "sound money," but "free silver," for free silver, so styled, meant a great booming of silver mining.

"We don't want him here," said these miners. "We have heard enough about him and his gold standard. He had better keep away, or he'll regret it."

When Theodore Roosevelt was told he might have trouble in the mining camps, he merely shrugged his shoulders.

"I know these men," he said. "The most of them are as honest and respectable as the citizens of New York. I am not afraid of the vicious element. The better class are bound to see fair play."

The governor spoke at a place called Armory Hall, and the auditorium was packed. He had just begun his speech when there was a wild yelling and cat-calling, all calculated to drown him out. He waited for a minute, and then, as the noise subsided, tried to go on once more, when a voice cried out:

"What about rotten beef?" referring to the beef furnished during the Santiago campaign, which had, of course, come through a Republican Commissary Department.

"I ate that beef," answered the governor, quickly. And then he added to the fellow who had thus questioned him: "You will never get near enough to be hit with a bullet, or within five miles of it." At this many burst into applause, and the man, who was a coward at heart, sneaked from the hall in a hurry.

He was no soldier and had never suffered the hardships of any campaign, and many hooted him as he deserved.

But the trouble was not yet over. Theodore Roosevelt finished his address, and then started to leave the hall in company with a number of his friends. On the way to the train a crowd of rowdies followed the candidate's party, and threw all sorts of things at them. One man made a personal attack on the governor and hit him on the chest with a stick. He tried to leap away, but was knocked down by a personal friend of Theodore Roosevelt.

"Down with the gold bugs!" was the cry, and the violence of the mob increased. The friends of Governor Roosevelt rallied to his support, and blows were given and taken freely. But with it all the candidate reached his train in safety, and in a few minutes more had left the town far behind. He was not much disturbed, and the very next day went on with his speech-making as if nothing out of the ordinary had happened. The better classes of citizens of Victor were much disturbed over the happening, and they sent many regrets to Governor Roosevelt, assuring him that such a demonstration would never again be permitted to occur.

CHAPTER XXII

ELECTED VICE-PRESIDENT OF THE UNITED STATES PRESIDES OVER THE SENATE TAX UPON THEODORE ROOSEVELT'S STRENGTH START ON ANOTHER GRAND HUNTING TOUR

But the campaign, sharp and bitter as it had been, was not yet at an end. In New York City there followed a "Sound Money Parade," which was perhaps the largest of its kind ever witnessed in the United States. It was composed of all sorts and conditions of men, from bankers and brokers of Wall Street to the humble factory and mill hands from up the river and beyond. The parade took several hours to pass, and was witnessed by crowds almost as great as had witnessed the Dewey demonstration.

In New York City, as the time drew closer for the election, there was every intimation that the contest would be an unusually "hot" one, and that there would be much bribery and corruption. It was said by some that police methods were very lax at that time, and that the saloons, which ought to be closed on election day, would be almost if not quite wide open.

PRESIDENT MCKINLEY AND VICE-PRESIDENT ROOSEVELT.
(*Photograph by Pach Bros., N.Y.*)

"We must have an honest election," said Governor Roosevelt. And without loss of time he sent letters to Mayor Van Wyck, and to the sheriff and the district attorney of the county of New York, calling their attention to the facts in the case, and telling them that he would hold them strictly responsible if they did not do their full duty. As a consequence the election was far more orderly than it might otherwise have been in the metropolitan district.

The results of the long contest were speedily known. McKinley and Roosevelt had been elected by a large plurality, and both they and their numerous friends and supporters were correspondingly happy. Great parades were had in their honor, and it was predicted, and rightly, that the prosperity which our country had enjoyed for several years in the past would continue for many years to come.

During those days the United States had but one outside difficulty, which was in China. There a certain set of people called the Boxers arose in rebellion and threatened the lives of all foreigners, including American citizens. An International Army was organized, including American, English, French, German, Japanese, and other troops, and a quick attack was made upon Tien-Tsin and Pekin, and the suffering foreigners in China were rescued. In this campaign the American soldiers did their full share of the work and added fresh laurels to the name of Old Glory.

The tax upon the strength of the newly elected Vice-President had been very great, and he was glad to surrender the duties of governor into the hands of his successor. But as Vice-President, Theodore Roosevelt became the presiding officer of the United States Senate, a position of equal if not greater importance.

As President of the Senate it is said that Mr. Roosevelt was kind yet firm, and ever on the alert to see that affairs ran smoothly. He occupied the position only for one short winter session, and during that time nothing came under discussion that was of prime importance, although my young readers must remember that all the work accomplished in our Senate is of more or less magnitude.

"He was very earnest in his work," says one who was in the Senate at that time. "As was his usual habit, he took little for granted, but usually started to investigate for himself. He knew the rules thoroughly, and rarely made an error."

For a long time the newly elected Vice-President had been wanting to get back to his favorite recreation, hunting. Despite the excitement of political life, he could not overcome his fondness for his rifle and the wilderness. He felt that an outing would do his system much good, and accordingly arranged for a five weeks' hunting trip in northwestern Colorado.

In this trip, which he has himself described in one of his admirable hunting papers, he had with him two companions, Dr. Gerald Webb of Colorado Springs, and Mr. Philip K. Stewart, an old friend who in former years had been captain of the Yale base-ball team.

The party went as far as the railroad would carry them, and then started for a settlement called Meeker, forty miles distant. The weather was extremely cold, with the thermometer from ten to twenty degrees below zero, but the journey to Meeker was made in safety, and here the hunters met their guide, a well-known hunter of that region named Goff, and started with him for his ranch, several miles away.

Theodore Roosevelt would have liked to bring down a bear on this trip, but the grizzlies were all in winter quarters and sleeping soundly, so the hunt was confined to bob-cats and cougars. The hunting began early, for on the way to the ranch the hounds treed a bob-cat, commonly known as a lynx, which was secured without much trouble, and a second bob-cat was secured the next day.

The territory surrounding Goff's ranch, called the Keystone, was an ideal one for hunting, with clumps of cottonwoods and pines scattered here and there, and numerous cliffs and ravines, the hiding-places of game unnumbered. The ranch home stood at the foot of several well-wooded hills, a long, low, one-story affair, built of rough logs, but clean and comfortable within.

The two days' ride in the nipping air had been a severe test of endurance, and all were glad, when the ranch was reached, to "thaw out" before the roaring fire, and sit down to the hot and hearty meal that had been prepared in anticipation of their coming.

The hunters had some excellent hounds, trained especially for bob-cats and cougars, animals that were never allowed to go after small game under any circumstances. Theodore Roosevelt was much taken with them from the start, and soon got to know each by name.

"In cougar hunting the success of the hunter depends absolutely upon his hounds," says Mr. Roosevelt. And he described each hound with great minuteness, showing that he allowed little to escape his trained eye while on this tour.

On the day after the arrival at the ranch the party went out for its first cougar, which, as my young readers perhaps know, is an animal inhabiting certain wild parts of our West and Southwest. The beast grows to a size of from six to nine feet in length, and weighs several hundred pounds. It is variously known as a puma and panther, the latter name sometimes being changed to "painter." When attacked, it is ofttimes exceedingly savage, and on certain occasions has been known to kill a man.

In Colorado the cougar is hunted almost exclusively with the aid of hounds, and this was the method adopted on the present occasion. With the pen of a true sportsman, Mr. Roosevelt tells us how the hounds were held back until a cougar trail less than thirty-six hours old was struck. Then off went the pack along the cliffs and ravines, with the hunters following on horseback. The trail led up the mountain side and then across the valley opposite, and soon the hounds were out of sight. Leading their steeds, the hunters went down the valley and followed the dogs, to find they had separated among the bare spots beyond. But soon came a welcome sound.

"The cougar's treed," announced the guide. And so it proved. But when the hunters came closer, the cougar, an old female, leaped from the tree, outdistanced the dogs, and leaped into another tree. Then, as the party again came up, the beast took another leap and started to run once more. But now the hounds were too quick, and in a trice they had the cougar surrounded. Slipping in, Theodore Roosevelt ended the struggles of the wild beast by a knife-thrust behind the shoulder.

The next day there was another hunt, and this had rather a tinge of sadness to it. The dogs tracked a mother cougar, who occupied her den with her three kittens. The hounds rushed into the hole, barking furiously, and presently one came out with a dead kitten in his mouth.

"I had supposed a cougar would defend her young to the last," says Mr. Roosevelt, "but such was not the case in this instance. For some minutes she kept the dogs at bay, but gradually gave ground, leaving her three kittens." The dogs killed the kittens without loss of time, and then followed the cougar as she fled from the other end of her hole. But the hounds were too quick for her, and soon had her on the ground. Theodore Roosevelt rushed up, knife in one hand and rifle in the other. With the firearm he struck the beast in the jaws, and then ended the struggle by a knife-thrust straight into the heart.

To many this may seem a cruel sport, and in a certain sense it assuredly is; but my young readers must remember that cougars and other wild beasts are a menace to civilization in the far West, and they have been shot down and killed at every available opportunity. More than this, as I have already mentioned, Theodore Roosevelt is more than a mere hunter delighting in bloodshed. He is a naturalist, and examines with care everything brought down and reports upon it, so that his hunting trips have added not a little to up-to-date natural history. The skulls of the various animals killed on this trip were forwarded to the Biological Survey, Department of Agriculture, Washington, and in return Mr. Roosevelt received a letter, part of which stated:

"Your series of skulls from Colorado is incomparably the largest, most complete, and most valuable series ever brought together from any single locality, and will be of inestimable value in determining the amount of individual variation."

CHAPTER XXIII

THE ROOSEVELT FAMILY IN THE ADIRONDACKS THE PAN-AMERICAN EXPOSITION AT BUFFALO SHOOTING OF PRESIDENT MCKINLEY THE VICE-PRESIDENT'S VISIT DEATH OF THE PRESIDENT

Theodore Roosevelt's companions of the hunt remained with him for fourteen days, after which they departed, leaving him with Goff, the ranchman and hunter already mentioned.

When the pair were alone, they visited Juniper Mountain, said to be a great ground for cougars and bob-cats, and there hunted with great success. All together the trip of five weeks' hunting netted fourteen cougars, the largest of which was eight feet in length and weighed 227 pounds. Mr. Roosevelt also brought down five bob-cats, showing that he was just as skilful with his rifle as ever.

The hero of San Juan Hill fairly loved the outdoor exercise of the hunt, and spent three weeks in keen enjoyment after his companions had departed. During this time it snowed heavily, so that the hunters were often compelled to remain indoors. As luck would have it there were other ranches in that vicinity, with owners that were hospitable, so that they did not have to go into camp, as would otherwise have been the case.

On the last day of the hunt, Theodore Roosevelt was able to bring down the largest cougar yet encountered. The hounds were on the trail of one beast when they came across that of another and took it up with but little warning.

"We're going to get a big one now," said Goff. "Just you wait and see."

"Well, if we do, it will be a good ending to my outing," responded Theodore Roosevelt.

The cougar was at last located by the hounds in a large pinyon on the side of a hill. It had run a long distance and was evidently out of breath, but as the hunters drew closer, it leaped to the ground and trotted away through the snow. Away went the hounds on the new trail of the beast.

"He's game, and he'll get away if he can," said the guide.

At the top of another hill the cougar halted and one of the hounds leaped in, and was immediately sent sprawling by a savage blow of the wild animal's paw. Then on went the cougar as before, the hounds barking wildly as they went in pursuit.

When Theodore Roosevelt came up once more, the cougar was in another pinyon tree, with the hounds in a semicircle on the ground below.

"Now I think I've got him," whispered Theodore Roosevelt to his companion, and advanced on foot, with great cautiousness. At first he could see nothing, but at last made out the back and tail of the great beast, as it lay crouched among the branches. With great care he took aim and fired, and the cougar fell to the ground, shot through the back.

At once the hounds rushed in and seized the game. But the cougar was not yet dead, and snapping and snarling the beast slipped over the ground and down a hillside, with the dogs all around it. Theodore Roosevelt came up behind, working his way through the brush with all speed. Then, watching his chance, he jumped in, hunting-knife in hand, and despatched the game.

"A good haul," cried Goff. And later on he and his men came to the conclusion that it was the same cougar that had carried off a cow and a steer and killed a work horse belonging to one of the ranches near by.

The five weeks spent in the far West strengthened Theodore Roosevelt a great deal, and it was with renewed energy that he took up his duties as Vice-President of our nation.

In the meantime, however, matters were not going on so well at home. Among the children two had been very sick, and in the summer it was suggested that some pure mountain air would do them a great deal of good.

"Very well, we'll go to the mountains," said Mr. Roosevelt, and looked around to learn what place would be best to choose.

Among the Adirondack Mountains of New York State there is a reservation of ninety-six thousand acres leased by what is called the Adirondack Club, a wealthy organization of people who have numerous summer cottages built within the preserve.

Among the members was a Mr. McNaughten, an old friend of the Roosevelt family, and he suggested that they occupy his cottage until the close of the season. This invitation was accepted, and the whole Roosevelt family moved up to the spot, which was located at the foot of Mount Marcy, the largest of the mountains in that vicinity. Here Mr. Roosevelt spent much time in hunting and fishing, and also in writing. The family were not forgotten, and he frequently went out with the whole party, rowing and exploring. Sometimes they took baskets of lunch with them and had regular picnics in the woods, something the Roosevelt children enjoyed very much.

In the meantime the Pan-American Exposition at Buffalo, New York, had been opened, and day after day it was thronged with visitors. Vice-President Roosevelt had assisted at the opening, and he was one of many who hoped the Exposition would be a great success.

At the Exposition our government had a large exhibit, and it was thought highly proper that President McKinley should visit the ground in his official capacity and deliver an address. Preparations were accordingly made, and the address was delivered on September 5 to a most enthusiastic throng.[3]

On the following day the President was driven to the Temple of Music, on the Exposition grounds, there to hold a public reception. The crowds were as great as ever, but perfectly orderly, and filed in at one side of the building and out at the other, each person in turn being permitted to grasp the Chief Magistrate's hand.

For a while all went well, and nobody noticed anything unusual about a somewhat weak-faced individual who joined the crowd, and who had one hand covered with a handkerchief. As this rascal came up to shake hands, he raised the hand with the handkerchief and, using a concealed pistol, fired two shots at President McKinley.

For an instant everybody was dazed. Then followed a commotion, and while some went to the wounded Executive's assistance, others leaped upon the dastardly assassin and made him a prisoner.

There was an excellent hospital upon the Exposition grounds, and to this President McKinley was carried. Here it was found that both bullets had entered his body, one having struck the breastbone and the other having entered the abdomen. The physicians present did all they possibly could for him, and then he was removed to the residence of Mr. Millburn, the President of the Exposition.

In the meantime, all unconscious of the awful happening that was to have such an influence upon his future, Mr. Roosevelt had been enjoying himself with his family, and helping to take care of the children that were not yet totally recovered from their illness. All seemed to be progressing finely, and he had gone off on a little tour to Vermont, to visit some points of interest and deliver a few addresses.

He was at Isle La Motte, not far from Burlington, when the news reached him that President McKinley had been shot. He had just finished an address, and for the moment he could not believe the sad news.

"Shot!" he said. "How dreadful!" And could scarcely say another word. He asked for the latest bulletin, and, forgetful of all else, took the first train he could get to Buffalo, and then hastened to the side of his Chief.

It was truly a sad meeting. For many years these two men had known each other, and they were warm friends. Their methods were somewhat different, but each stood for what was just and right and true, and each was ready to give his country his best service, no matter what the cost.

It was a sad time for the whole nation, and men and women watched the bulletins eagerly, hoping and praying that President McKinley might recover. Every hour there was some slight change, and people would talk it over in a whisper.

In a few days there were hopeful signs, and the physicians, deceived by them, said they thought the President would recover. This was glad news to Theodore Roosevelt. Yet he lingered on, fearful to go away, lest the news should prove untrue and he should be needed. But then there was a still brighter turn, and he thought of his own family, and of the fact that one of his children was again ill.

"I will return to my family," said he to two of his closest friends. "But if I am needed here, let me know at once." And his friends promised to keep him informed. Two days later he was back among the Adirondacks, in the bosom of his family.

The prayers of a whole nation were in vain. William McKinley's mission on earth was finished, and one week after he was shot he breathed his last. His wife came to bid him farewell, and so did his other relatives, and his friend of many years, Mark Hanna, and the members of his Cabinet.

"It is God's way," murmured the dying Executive. "His will be done, not ours." Then like a child going to sleep, he relapsed into unconsciousness, from which he did not recover. He died September 14, 1901, at a little after two o'clock in the morning.

It was the last of a truly great life. Illustrious men may come and go, but William McKinley will be remembered so long as our nation endures. As a soldier and a statesman he gave his best talents to better the conditions of his fellow-creatures, and to place the United States where we justly belong, among the truly great nations of the world.

CHAPTER XXIV

THEODORE ROOSEVELT'S TRAMP UP MOUNT MARCY A MESSAGE OF IMPORTANCE WILD MIDNIGHT RIDE THROUGH THE MOUNTAINS ON THE SPECIAL TRAINS FROM NORTH CREEK TO BUFFALO

With a somewhat lighter heart, Theodore Roosevelt returned to the Adirondacks and joined his family on Wednesday, three days previous to President McKinley's death. The last report he had received from Buffalo was the most encouraging of any, and he now felt almost certain that the President would survive the outrageous attack that had been made upon his person.

"He will get well," said several who lived close by. "You need not worry about his condition any longer."

On the following day it was planned to go up to Colton Lake, five miles from where the family was stopping. Some friends went along, and in the party were Mrs. Roosevelt and several of the children. Two guides accompanied them, and it was decided to spend the night at a camp on the lake, returning home the following day.

The next morning it rained, but in spite of this drawback Theodore Roosevelt, leaving the ladies and children to return to the cottage, started to climb Mount Marcy. Such an undertaking was exactly to his liking, and he went up the rough and uneven trail with the vigor of a trained woodsman, the guide leading the way and the other gentlemen of the party following.

At last, high up on the side of Mount Marcy, the party reached a small body of water known as Tear of the Clouds, and here they rested for lunch.

"You are certainly a great walker, Mr. Roosevelt," remarked one of the gentlemen during the progress of the lunch.

"Oh, I have to be," answered Theodore Roosevelt, jokingly. "A Vice-President needs exercise to keep him alive. You see, when he is in the Senate, all of his work is done sitting down."

The words had scarcely been uttered when one of the party pointed to a man climbing up the mountain side toward them. The newcomer held some yellow telegram-slips in his hand, and Theodore Roosevelt quickly arose to receive them.

He had soon mastered the contents of the messages. President McKinley was much worse; it was likely that he would not live. For fully a minute Mr. Roosevelt did not speak. He realized the great responsibility which rested upon his shoulders. Then, in a voice filled with emotion, he read the messages aloud.

"Gentlemen," he continued, "I must return to the club-house at once." And without waiting, he turned and started down the mountain side along the trail by which he had come.

It was a long, hard walk, but it is doubtful if Theodore Roosevelt took note of it. A thousand thoughts must have flashed through his mind. If William McKinley should indeed breathe his last, the nation would look to him as their Chief Magistrate. He could not make himself believe that his President was to die.

It was not long before Theodore Roosevelt reached the club-house at the lake. He asked for further news, but none was forthcoming.

"We will send to the lower club-house at once," said his friends. "You had better take a short rest, in case you have a sudden call to make the trip to Buffalo."

A misty rain was falling, and the atmosphere of the mountains was raw and penetrating. Messengers were quickly despatched to the lower club-house, and by eleven o'clock that evening news came back that left no doubt of the true condition of affairs. President McKinley was sinking rapidly, and his death was now only a question of a few hours.

"I must go, and at once," said Theodore Roosevelt. And soon a light wagon drove up to the club-house, and he leaped in. There was a short good-by to his family and his friends, the whip cracked, and the drive of thirty-five miles to the nearest railroad station was begun.

It was a never-to-be-forgotten journey. For ten miles or more the road was fearfully rough and ran around the edges of overhanging cliffs, where a false turn might mean death. Then at times the road went down into deep hollows and over rocky hills. All was pitch black, save for the tiny yellow light hanging over the dashboard of the turnout. Crouched on the seat, Mr. Roosevelt urged the driver to go on, and go on they did, making better time during that rain and darkness than had before been made in broad daylight.

At last a place called Hunter's was reached, and Theodore Roosevelt alighted.

"What news have you for me?" he asked of a waiting messenger, and the latest message was handed to him. There was no new hope, President McKinley was sinking faster than ever. New horses were obtained, and the second part of the journey, from Hunter's to Aiden Lair, was begun.

And during that wild, swift ride of nine miles, when it seemed to Theodore Roosevelt as if he were racing against death, the angel of Life Everlasting claimed William McKinley, and the man crouched in the wagon, wet from the rain, hurrying to reach him, became the next President of the United States.

It was a little after three in the morning when Aiden Lair was reached. The sufferer at Buffalo had breathed his last, but Theodore Roosevelt did not know it, and he still hoped for the best. More fresh horses, and now the last sixteen miles of the rough journey were made on a buckboard. In spots the road was worse than it had previously been, and the driver was tempted to go slow.

"Go on!" cried Mr. Roosevelt, and held his watch in hand. "Go on!" And the driver obeyed, the buckboard dancing up and down over the rocks and swinging dangerously from side to side around the curves of ravines. But Theodore Roosevelt's mind was not on the road nor on the peril of that ride, but in that room in Buffalo where the great tragedy had just seen its completion.

At last, a little after five in the morning, the turnout came in sight of the railroad station at North Creek. A special train was in waiting for him. He gazed anxiously at the little knot of people assembled. Their very faces told him the sorrowful truth. President McKinley was dead.

With bowed head he entered a private car of the special train, and without delay the train started on its journey southward for Albany. No time was lost on this portion of the trip, and at seven o'clock Theodore Roosevelt reached the city in which but a short time before he had presided as Governor of the State.

At Albany he was met by Secretary of State Hay, who informed him officially that President McKinley was no more. He likewise informed the Vice-President that, considering the excitement, it might be best that Mr. Roosevelt be sworn in as President without delay.

Another special train was in waiting at Albany, and this was rushed westward with all possible speed, arriving in Buffalo at half-past one in the afternoon. In order to avoid the tremendous crowd at the Union railroad station, Mr. Roosevelt alighted at the Terrace station. Here he was met by several friends with a carriage and also a detachment of the Fourth Signal Corps and a squad of mounted police.

Without loss of time Theodore Roosevelt was driven to the Millburn house. Here he found a great many friends and relatives of the dead President assembled. All were too shocked over what had occurred to say much, and shook the hand of the coming President in silence.

Thousands of eyes were upon Theodore Roosevelt, but he noticed them not. Entering the Millburn house, he thought only of the one who had surrendered his life while doing his duty, and of that kind and patient woman now left to fight the battles of this world alone. He offered what consolation he could to Mrs. McKinley, heard the little that had not yet been told of that final struggle to fight off death, and then took his departure, to assume the high office thus suddenly and unexpectedly thrust upon him.

CHAPTER XXV

TAKES THE OATH AS PRESIDENT THE NEW CHIEF MAGISTRATE AT THE FUNERAL OF PRESIDENT MCKINLEY AT THE WHITE HOUSE HOW THE FIRST REAL WORKING DAY WAS SPENT

The new President took the oath of office at the residence of Mr. Ansley Wilcox in Buffalo. It is a fine, substantial mansion and has ever since been of historic interest to sight-seers.

When he arrived at the Wilcox home, he found a number of members of the McKinley Cabinet awaiting him, as well as Judge John R. Hazel, of the United States District Court, who administered the oath; and ten or a dozen others.

The scene was truly an affecting one. Secretary Root could scarcely control himself, for, twenty years before, he had been at a similar scene, when Vice-President Arthur became Chief Magistrate, after the assassination of President Garfield. In a voice filled with emotion he requested Vice-President Roosevelt, on behalf of the Cabinet as a whole, to take the prescribed oath.

It is recorded by an eye-witness that Theodore Roosevelt was pale, and that his eyes were dim with tears, as he stepped forward to do as bidden. His hand was uplifted, and then in a solemn voice the judge began the oath:

"I do solemnly swear that I will faithfully execute the office of President of the United States, and will, to the best of my ability, preserve, protect, and defend the Constitution of the United States."

The words were repeated in a low but distinct voice by Theodore Roosevelt, and a moment of utter silence followed.

"Mr. President, please attach your signature," went on the judge. And in a firm hand the new Chief Executive wrote "Theodore Roosevelt" at the bottom of the all-important document which made him the President of our beloved country.

Standing in that room, the President felt the great responsibility which now rested on his shoulders, and turning to those before him, he spoke as follows:

"In this hour of deep and terrible bereavement, I wish to state that it shall be my aim to continue absolutely unbroken the policy of President McKinley for the peace and prosperity and honor of our country."

These were no mere words, as his actions immediately afterward prove. On reaching Washington he assembled the Cabinet at the home of Commander Cowles, his brother-in-law, and there spoke to them somewhat in this strain:

"I wish to make it clear to you, gentlemen, that what I said at Buffalo I meant. I want each of you to remain as a member of my Cabinet. I need your advice and counsel. I tender you the office in the same manner that I would tender it if I were entering upon the discharge of my duties as the result of an election by the people." Having thus declared himself, the newly made President asked each member personally to stay with him. It was a sincere request, and the Cabinet members all agreed to remain by Mr. Roosevelt and aid him exactly as they had been aiding Mr. McKinley. Thus was it shown to the world at large, and especially to the anarchists, of which the assassin of McKinley had been one, that though the President might be slain, the government still lived.

The entire country was prostrate over the sudden death of President McKinley, and one of the first acts of Theodore Roosevelt, after assuming the responsibilities of his office, was to issue the following proclamation:

"A terrible bereavement has befallen our people. The President of the United States has been struck down; a crime committed not only against the Chief Magistrate, but against every law-abiding and liberty-loving citizen.

"President McKinley crowned a life of largest love for his fellow-men, of most earnest endeavor for their welfare, by a death of Christian fortitude; and both the way in which he lived his life and the way in which, in the supreme hour of trial, he met his death, will remain forever a precious heritage of our people.

"It is meet that we, as a nation, express our abiding love and reverence for his life, our deep sorrow for his untimely death.

"Now, therefore, I, Theodore Roosevelt, President of the United States, do appoint Thursday next, September 19, the day in which the body of the dead President will be laid in its last earthly resting-place, a day of mourning and prayer throughout the United States.

"I earnestly recommend all the people to assemble on that day in their respective places of divine worship, there to bow down in submission to the will of Almighty God, and to pay out of full hearts their homage of love and reverence to the great and good President whose death has smitten the nation with bitter grief."

The funeral of President McKinley was a most imposing one. The body was at first laid in state in the City Hall at Buffalo, where President Roosevelt and fully a hundred and fifty thousand men, women, and children went to view the remains. From Buffalo the remains were taken by special funeral train to Washington, and there placed in the Rotunda of the Capitol. Here the crowd was equally great, and here the services were attended by representatives from almost every civilized nation on the globe. Outside a marine band was stationed, playing the dead President's favorite hymns, "Lead, Kindly Light" and "Nearer, my God, to Thee," and in the singing of these thousands of mourners joined, while the tears of sorrow streamed down their faces.

From Washington the body of the martyred President was taken to Canton, Ohio, where had been his private home. Here his friends and neighbors assembled to do him final honor, and great arches of green branches and flowers were erected, under which the funeral cortege passed. As the body was placed in the receiving vault, business throughout the entire United States was suspended. In spirit, eighty millions of people were surrounding the mortal clay left by the passing of a soul to the place whence it had come. It was truly a funeral of which the greatest of kings might well be proud.

The taking-off of President McKinley undoubtedly had a great effect upon President Roosevelt. During the Presidential campaign the Vice-Presidential nominee had made many speeches in behalf of his fellow candidate, showing the high personal character of McKinley, and what might be expected from the man in case he was elected once more to the office of Chief Magistrate. More than this, when Assistant Secretary of the Navy, Mr. Roosevelt had done his best to carry out the plans formulated by the President. The two were close friends, and in the one brief session of the Senate when he was Vice-President, Mr. Roosevelt gave to President McKinley many evidences of his high regard.

On returning to Washington, President Roosevelt did not at once take up his residence at the White House, preferring that the place should be left to Mrs. McKinley until she had sufficiently recovered from her terrible shock to arrange for the removal of the family's personal effects.

As it may interest some of my young readers to know how President Roosevelt's first day as an active President was spent, I append the following, taken down at the time by a reporter for a press association:

"Reached the White House from Canton, on September 20, 1901, at 9.40 A.M. Went at once to the private office formerly occupied by President McKinley, and, as speedily as possible, settled down for the business of the day.

"Met Secretary Long of the navy in the cabinet room and held a discussion concerning naval matters; received Colonel Sanger to talk over some army appointments; signed appointments of General J. M. Bell and others; met Senators Cullom and Proctor.

"At 11 A.M. called for the first time formal meeting of the Cabinet and transacted business of that body until 12.30 P.M.

"Received his old friend, General Wood, and held conference with him and with Secretary Root in regard to Cuban election laws.

"President Roosevelt left the White House at 1.20 P.M. to take lunch with Secretary Hay at the latter's residence. He was alone, disregarding the services of a body-guard.

"Returned to the White House at 3.30 P.M. and transacted business with some officials and received a few personal friends.

"Engaged with Secretary Cortelyou from 4 P.M. to 6.30 P.M. in the transaction of public business, disposal of mail, etc.

"Left the White House unattended at 6.30 P.M. and walked through the semi-dark streets of Washington to 1733 N Street, N.W., the residence of his brother-in-law, Commander Cowles. Dined in private with the family.

"Late in the evening received a few close friends. Retired at 11 P.M."

It will be observed that special mention is made of the fact that President Roosevelt travelled around alone. Immediately after the terrible tragedy at Buffalo many citizens were of the opinion that the Chief Magistrate of our nation ought to be strongly protected, for fear of further violence, but to this Theodore Roosevelt would not listen.

"I am not afraid," he said calmly. "We are living in a peaceful country, and the great mass of our people are orderly, law-abiding citizens. I can trust them, and take care of myself." And to this he held, despite the protestations of his closest friends. Of course he is scarcely ever without some guard or secret service detective close at hand, but no outward display of such protection is permitted. And let it be added to the credit of our people that, though a few cranks and crazy persons have caused him a little annoyance, he has never, up to the present time, been molested in any way.

CHAPTER XXVI

CONTINUING THE WORK BEGUN BY PRESIDENT MCKINLEY THE PANAMA CANAL AGITATION VISIT OF PRINCE HENRY OF PRUSSIA THE PRESIDENT AT THE CHARLESTON EXPOSITION

President Roosevelt had said he would continue the policy inaugurated by President McKinley, and one of the important steps in this direction was to appoint many to office who had been expecting appointment at the hands of the martyred President. This gained him many friends, and soon some who had kept themselves at a distance flocked around, to aid him in every possible manner.

Late in September the last of the McKinley effects were taken from the White House, and some days later the newly made President moved in, with his family, who had come down from the Adirondacks some time previous. In Washington the family were joined by Mr. Roosevelt's two brothers-in-law, Commander Wm. Sheffield Cowles and Mr. Douglas Robinson, and their wives, and the relatives remained together for some days.

It was at first feared by some politicians that President Roosevelt would be what is termed a "sectional President," that is, that he would favor one section of our country to the exclusion of the others, but he soon proved that he was altogether too noble for such baseness.

"I am going to be President of the whole United States," he said. "I don't care for sections or sectional lines. I was born in the North, but my mother was from the South, and I have spent much of my time in the West, so I think I can fairly represent the whole country."

President Roosevelt sympathized deeply with the condition of the negroes in the South, and for the purpose of learning the true state of affairs sent for Mr. Booker T. Washington, one of the foremost colored men of this country and founder of the

Tuskegee Industrial School for Colored People. They had a long conference at the White House, which Mr. Washington enjoyed very much. For this action many criticised the President severely, but to this he paid no attention, satisfied that he had done his duty as his conscience dictated.

PRESIDENT ROOSEVELT AT HIS DESK.

President Roosevelt's first message to Congress was awaited with considerable interest. It was remembered that he was the youngest Executive our White House had ever known, and many were curious to know what he would say and what he proposed to do.

The Fifty-seventh Congress of the United States assembled at Washington, December 2, 1901, and on the day following, President Roosevelt's first annual message was read in both Senate and House of Representatives.

It proved to be a surprisingly long and strong state paper, and by many was considered one of the best messages sent to Congress in many years. It touched upon general conditions in our country, spoke for improvements in the army and the navy, called for closer attention to civil service reform, for a correction of the faults in the post-office system, and for a clean administration in the Philippines, Hawaii, and Porto Rico. It spoke of several great needs of the government, and added that the Gold Standard Act had been found timely and judicious.

"President Roosevelt is all right," was the general comment, after the message had been printed in the various papers of our country. "He is looking ahead, and he knows exactly what this country wants and needs. We are prosperous now, and if we want to continue so, we must keep our hands on the plough, and not look backward."

The first break in the old Cabinet occurred on December 17, when Postmaster General Charles E. Smith resigned. His place was immediately filled by the appointment of Henry C. Payne, of Wisconsin. Soon after this Secretary Gage of the Treasury resigned, and his place was filled by former governor Leslie M. Shaw, of Iowa.

For a long time there had been before the American people various suggestions to build a canal across Central America, to join the Atlantic and the Pacific oceans, so that the ships wanting to go from one body of water to the other would not have to take the long and expensive trip around Cape Horn.

In years gone by the French had also contemplated such a canal, and had even gone to work at the Isthmus of Panama, making an elaborate survey and doing not a little digging. But the work was beyond them, and the French Canal Company soon ran out of funds and went into the hands of a receiver.

"We ought to take hold and dig a canal," was heard on all sides in the United States. But where to dig the canal was a question. Some said the Isthmus of Panama was the best place, while others preferred a route through Nicaragua. The discussion waxed very warm, and at last a Commission was appointed to go over both routes and find out which would be the more satisfactory from every point of view.

The Commission was not very long in reaching a decision. The Panama Canal Company was willing to sell out all its interest in the work already done for forty millions of dollars, and it was recommended that the United States accept this offer. President Roosevelt received the report, and lost no time in submitting it to Congress.

At the beginning of the new year, 1902, there was a grand ball at the White House, attended by a large gathering of people, including many of the foreign representatives accredited to Washington. The occasion was the introduction into society of Miss Alice Roosevelt, and the affair was a most pleasing one from beginning to end.

One of the President's sons, Theodore Roosevelt, Jr., had been sent to a boarding school at Groton, Massachusetts. Early in February he was taken down with a cold that developed into pneumonia. It looked as if the youth might die, and both Mrs. Roosevelt and the President lost no time in leaving Washington and going to his bedside. The sympathy of the whole country was with the anxious parents, and when it was announced that the crisis had been passed in safety there was much relief in all quarters.

Before this illness occurred there came to the Roosevelts an invitation which pleased them, and especially Miss Alice, not a little. The German Emperor William was having a yacht built in this country, at Shooter's Island. He sent his brother, Prince Henry of Prussia, over to attend the launching, and requested Miss Roosevelt to christen the yacht, which was to be called the *Meteor*.

The arrival of Prince Henry was made a gala day by many who wished to see the friendship between the United States and Germany more firmly cemented than ever, and the royal visitor was treated with every consideration wherever he went. From New York he journeyed to Washington, where he dined with the President. He returned to New York with President Roosevelt and with Miss Roosevelt, and on February 25 the launching occurred, in the presence of thousands of people and a great many craft of all sorts. Miss Roosevelt performed the christening in appropriate style, and this was followed by music from a band and the blowing of hundreds of steam whistles. After these ceremonies were over, there followed an elaborate dinner given by the mayor of New York, and then the Prince started on a tour of the country lasting two weeks. His visit made a good impression wherever he went, and he was universally put down as a right good fellow.

It was about this time that President Roosevelt showed he was not to be led altogether by what his party did. So far he had not vetoed any measures sent to him for his signature. Now, however, a bill came to him touching the desertion of a sailor in the navy. Congress was willing to strike the black record of the sailor from the books, but President Roosevelt would not have it.

"The sailor did wrong," he said. "He knew what he was doing, too. The record against him must stand." And he vetoed the bill. On the other hand he was prompt to recognize real worth in those who had served the government, and when over two hundred private pension bills came before him for his approval, he signed them without a murmur.

The people of Charleston, South Carolina, had been arranging for a long time to hold an exposition which should set forth the real advance and worth of the leading southern industries. This exposition was now open to the public, and President Roosevelt and his wife were invited to attend the exhibit. With so much southern blood in his veins, the President could not think of refusing, and he and Mrs. Roosevelt visited the exposition early in April.

It was a gala day at Charleston, and the President and Mrs. Roosevelt were received with every honor due their rank, and with great personal consideration. Governor McSweeney of the state was assisted by Governor Aycock, of North Carolina, in receiving President Roosevelt.

A stirring patriotic speech was made by the President during his visit, and a feature of the trip was the presentation of a sword to Major Micah Jenkins of the Rough Riders. A great number of President Roosevelt's former troopers were present, and all were glad, as of old, to crowd around and take him by the hand.

CHAPTER XXVII

DESTRUCTION OF ST. PIERRE AMERICAN AID THE GREAT COAL STRIKE PRESIDENT ROOSEVELT ENDS THE DIFFICULTY TOUR THROUGH NEW ENGLAND THE TROLLEY ACCIDENT IN THE BERKSHIRES A PROVIDENTIAL ESCAPE FROM DEATH

During the summer of 1902 two matters of great importance occurred in which the whole people of our nation were deeply interested.

Early in May occurred tremendous volcanic eruptions on the islands of Martinique and St. Vincent. At the former island, Mont Pelee threw such a rain of fire upon the town of St. Pierre that the entire place, with about thirty thousand people, was wiped out of existence in a minute. At other points the eruptions were not so bad, yet hundreds lost their lives, and all of the islands of the Lesser Antilles were thrown into a state bordering upon panic.

It was felt that something must be done, and at once, for the sufferers, and a large fund for relief was gathered, of which the Americans contributed their full share. The volcanic disturbances continued for some time, and as it was thought they might also cover certain portions of Central America, nothing was done further concerning a canal to unite the two oceans.

The other event of importance was the strike of thousands upon thousands of coal-miners, working in Pennsylvania and other states. The miners did not think they were being treated rightly and went out in a body, and for many weeks not a pound of coal of any kind was mined. This produced a double hardship, for people could get no coal either for the fall or winter, and the miners were, in some cases, reduced almost to the verge of starvation. Neither the workmen nor the operators of the mines would give in, and soon there was more or less violence, and some soldiers had to be called out in an effort to preserve order.

As matters went from bad to worse, and it looked as if the entire eastern section of our country would have to go without coal for the winter, there were loud demands that the government take hold of the difficulty and settle the matter, if not in one way, then in another.

At last, early in October, the whole country was aroused, for it was felt that with no coal a winter of untold suffering stared the people in the face. President Roosevelt held a conference at Washington with the mine operators and the representatives of the miners.

"We must get together, gentlemen," said he. "The country cannot do without coal, and you must supply it to us." And he laid down the law in a manner not to be misunderstood.

Another conference followed, and then a third, and at last the coal operators asked the President to appoint a Commission to decide upon the points in dispute. To this the representative of the mine workers agreed, and as a result a Commission was appointed by President Roosevelt, which was to settle all points in dispute, and by its decision each side was to abide. In the meantime, while the Commission was at work, the mine workers were to resume their labors. The mines were thereupon once more put in operation, after a strike lasting over five months. This is the greatest coal strike known in American history, and it is not likely that the people at large will ever again permit themselves to suffer for the want of coal as they did during that fall and the winter which followed.

Early in June occurred the centennial celebration of the founding of the United States Military Academy at West

Point. The occasion was made one of great interest, and among the many distinguished visitors were President Roosevelt and General Miles, head of our army at that time. The President reviewed the cadets and made a speech to them, complimenting them on their truly excellent showing as soldiers.

Although very busy with matters of state, President Roosevelt received an urgent call to deliver a Fourth of July oration at Pittsburg. He consented, and spoke to a vast assemblage on the rights and duties of American citizens.

To remain in Washington during the hot summer months was out of the question with President Roosevelt and his family, and early in the season he removed to Oyster Bay, there to enjoy himself as best he might during the short time allowed him for recreation.

That the business of the administration might not be too seriously interrupted, he hired a few rooms over a bank building in the village of Oyster Bay, and these were fitted up for himself and his several secretaries and assistants. To the bank building he rode or drove every day, spending an hour or more over the routine work required. By this means undesirable visitors were kept away from his private residence, and he was permitted to enjoy himself as he pleased in company with his family.

While Mr. Roosevelt was summering at Oyster Bay, it was arranged that he should make a short tour through New England, to last from August 22 to September 3. The trip covered every New England State, and was one of great pleasure to the President until the last day. Everywhere he went he was greeted by enthusiastic crowds, and, of course, had to make one of his characteristic speeches, accompanied by a great deal of hand-shaking.

On the last day of the trip he was at Dalton, Massachusetts, the home of Governor Crane. It had been planned to drive from Dalton to Lenox, a beautiful spot, adjoining Laurel Lake, where are located the summer homes of many American millionnaires.

The trip was begun without a thought of what was to follow. In the party, besides President Roosevelt, were Governor Crane, Secretary Cortelyou (afterward made a member of the Cabinet), United States Secret Service officer William Craig, and the driver of the carriage. It may be mentioned here that William Craig was detailed as a special guard for the President, and had been with him since the tour was begun.

There are a number of trolley lines in this section of Massachusetts, all centring in Pittsfield. As the mass of the people were very anxious to see President Roosevelt, the trolleys going to the points where he would pass were crowded, and the cars were run with more than usual speed.

As the carriage containing the President and his companions attempted to cross the trolley tracks a car came bounding along at a rapid rate of speed. There seemed to be no time in which to stop the car, and in an instant the long and heavy affair crashed into the carriage with all force, hurling the occupants to the street in all directions. The Secret Service officer, William Craig, was instantly killed, and the driver of the carriage was seriously hurt.

There was immediate and great excitement, and for the time being it was feared that President Roosevelt had been seriously injured. He had been struck a sharp blow on the leg, and had fallen on his face, cutting it not a little. The shock was a severe one, but in a little while he was himself once more, although his face was much swollen. Later still a small abscess formed on the injured limb, but this was skilfully treated by his physician, and soon disappeared. The others in the carriage escaped with but a few bruises and a general shaking-up.

The result of this accident, small as it was to the President personally, showed well how firmly he was seated in the affection of his fellow-citizens. From all over the country, as well as from his friends in foreign climes, telegrams of congratulation came pouring in. Everybody was glad that he had escaped, and everybody wished to show how he felt over the affair.

"President Roosevelt was much affected by the messages received," said one who was in a position to know. "It showed him that his friends were in every walk of life, from the highest to the lowest. Had he met death, as did the Secret Service officer detailed to guard over him, the shock to the people, coming so soon after the assassination of President McKinley, would have been tremendous."

The President had already been persuaded to consent to a short trip to the South, from September 5 to 10, and then a trip to the West, lasting until September 19, or longer. The trips came to an end on September 23, in Indiana, because of the abscess on the lower limb already mentioned, yet on November 19 he was given a grand reception by the people of Memphis, Tennessee, who flocked around him and were glad to see him as well as ever.

"We are so glad you escaped from that trolley accident!" was heard a hundred times.

"We can't afford to lose you, Mr. President," said others. "Really good men are too scarce." And then a cheer would go up for "The hero of San Juan Hill!"

His speeches on these trips were largely about the trusts and monopolies that are trying to control various industries of our country. It is an intricate subject, yet it can be said that Mr. Roosevelt understands it as well as any one, and is laboring hard to do what is right and best, both for the consumer and the capitalist.

Congress had, some time before, voted a large sum for the extension and improvement of the White House, and while Mr. Roosevelt and his family were at Oyster Bay these improvements were begun. They continued during the fall, and the President made his temporary home at a private residence in the capital city. Here it was he was treated for his wounded limb, and here he ended the coal strike, as already chronicled.

CHAPTER XXVIII

NEW OFFICES AT THE WHITE HOUSE SENDS A WIRELESS MESSAGE TO KING EDWARD OF ENGLAND END OF THE TROUBLE IN VENEZUELA THE CANADIAN BOUNDARY DISPUTE BEGINNING OF A TRIP TO THE WEST IN YELLOWSTONE PARK

The end of the year found President Roosevelt in the best of health, despite the accident some weeks previous. The improvements at the White House were now complete, and the family of the Chief Magistrate took possession. A separate set of offices for the President and his Cabinet had been built at the western end of the executive mansion, and the rooms formerly used for this purpose were turned into living apartments. The changes made have been approved by many who have seen them, and they have wondered why the alterations were not made a long time ago.

On December 1, Congress assembled for a new session, and on the day following the President's message was read. It was a masterly state paper, dealing with the trust question, our relations with the new government of Cuba (for the island was now free, just as we had meant it to be when the war with Spain started), the creation of a new department of Commerce and Labor, needs of the army and navy, and the all-important matter of how the Philippines should be governed. It may be added here that not long after this a Department of Commerce and Labor was created by Congress, and Mr. George B. Cortelyou, the secretary to the President, became its first official head. When Mr. Cortelyou left his post as secretary, Mr. William Loeb, Jr., who had been the President's private secretary for some time, became the regular first secretary to the Chief Magistrate, a place he occupies to-day.

Just about this time there was considerable trouble in Indianola, Mississippi. A colored young lady had been appointed postmistress, and the people in that vicinity refused to recognize her. The Post-Office Department did what it could in the matter, and then referred the case to the President.

THE WHITE HOUSE, SHOWING NEW OFFICES.

"As she has been regularly appointed, the people will have to accept her," said Mr. Roosevelt. And when there was more trouble, he sent forward an order that the post-office be shut up entirely. This was done, and for a long time the people of that vicinity had to get their mail elsewhere, a great inconvenience to them.

On January 1, 1903, the new cable to the Hawaiian Islands was completed, and President Roosevelt received a message from Governor Dole, and sent a reply to the same. About two weeks later the President sent a wireless, or rather cableless, message to King Edward of England. This helped to mark the beginning of a new era in message-sending which may cause great changes in the transmission of messages in the future.

For some time past there had been a small-sized war going on in Venezuela, South America, between that nation on one hand and England, Germany, and Italy on the other. This war had caused much disturbance to American trade. Pressure was brought to bear upon the several nations through President Roosevelt, and at last it was agreed to leave matters to be settled by arbitration at The Hague. The agreements to this end were signed at Washington, much to the President's satisfaction. All trouble then ceased, and American commerce was resumed as before.

For many years there had been a dispute between the United States and Canada, regarding a certain boundary line. This country claimed a long strip of territory next to the sea, near the seaports of Dyea and Skagway, and Canada claimed that this strip, about thirty miles in width, belonged to her domain.

There had been endless disputes about the claim, and considerable local trouble, especially during the rush to the Klondike after gold.

Many Americans contended that we had absolute right to the territory, and when arbitration was spoken of, said we had nothing to arbitrate. This was, in the main, President Roosevelt's view of the matter, yet, as things grew more disturbed, he realized, as a good business man, that something must be done. We did not wish to fight Canada and England for the strip of land, and neither did they wish to fight, so at last a Board of Arbitration was agreed upon, and the claims of both parties were carefully investigated. In the end nearly every point claimed by the United States was granted to us. It was a great satisfaction to have this long-standing dispute settled; and how much better it was to do it by arbitration than by going to war.

The regular session of Congress came to an end on March 4, 1903, but President Roosevelt had already called an extra session, to consider a bill for reciprocity in our dealing with the new government of Cuba and to ratify a treaty with Colombia concerning the Panama Canal.

There was a great deal of debating at this session of Congress. The bill concerning Cuba caused but little trouble, but many wanted the canal placed in Nicaragua instead of Panama, and did not wish to pay the forty millions of dollars asked for the work already accomplished by the old French Canal Company. But in the end the bill passed the United States Senate by a vote of seventy-three to five, with the proviso that should we fail to make a satisfactory arrangement about the Panama Canal, then the government should build the canal through Nicaragua. President Roosevelt was enthusiastic over a canal at the isthmus, and lost no time in arranging to push the work further.

The people of the far West were very anxious to meet the chief ruler of our nation, and early in the year it was arranged that President Roosevelt should leave Washington on April 1 for a tour to last until June. In that time he was to visit more than twenty States, and make over one hundred stops. The people in the West awaited his coming with much pleasure.

The President was justly entitled to this outing, for the nation was now at peace with the entire world, and never had business been so prosperous. More than this, our affairs with other nations had been so handled that throughout the entire civilized world no ruler was more popular than was Theodore Roosevelt. In England he was spoken of with the highest praise, and the regards of the Germans had already been shown in the visit of Prince Henry to this country. He was known to be vigorous to the last degree, but it was likewise realized that he was thoroughly honest and straight-forward.

The first stop of the President in his trip West was made at Chicago, where during the day he laid the corner-stone of the new law building of the University of Chicago, which university conferred upon him the degree of LL.D. (Doctor of Laws). In the evening he addressed an unusually large crowd at the Auditorium building, speaking upon the Monroe Doctrine.

From Chicago the President journeyed to Milwaukee, and then to St. Paul and Minneapolis. At the first-named city he made a forceful address on the trusts, giving his hearers a clear idea of how the great corporations of to-day were brought into existence, and what may be done to control them, and in the last-named city he spoke on the ever-important question of tariff.

It was an eventful week, and when Sunday came the Chief Magistrate was glad enough to take a day of rest at Sioux Falls, South Dakota. From there he journeyed to Gardiner, Montana, one of the entrances to that greatest of all American wonderlands, Yellowstone Park.

It was understood that President Roosevelt wished to visit the Park without a great following of the general public, and this wish was carried out to the letter. Mr. Roosevelt had with him the well-known naturalist, Mr. John Burroughs, and for about two weeks he enjoyed himself to his heart's content, visiting many of the spots of interest and taking it easy whenever he felt so disposed. It was not a hunting trip, although big game is plentiful enough in the Park. It was just getting "near to nature's heart," and Mr. Roosevelt afterward declared it to be one of the best outings he had ever experienced.

CORTELYOU. KNOX. PAYNE. MOODY. HAY. ROOSEVELT.
HITCHCOCK. ROOT. SHAW. WILSON.
PRESIDENT ROOSEVELT AND CABINET, 1903.

CHAPTER XXIX

DEDICATION OF THE FAIR BUILDINGS AT ST. LOUIS CONTINUATION OF THE TRIP TO SAN FRANCISCO UP IN THE FAR NORTH-WEST BACK IN WASHINGTON THE POST-OFFICE SCANDALS THE NEW REPUBLIC OF PANAMA A CANAL AT LAST PROCLAMATION REGARDING THE WAR BETWEEN JAPAN AND RUSSIA OPENING OF THE GREAT FAIR

After the refreshing tour of Yellowstone Park, President Roosevelt journeyed across Nebraska to Omaha, then across Iowa to Keokuk, and from the latter city to St. Louis.

As before, he delivered a number of addresses, and wherever he spoke great crowds came to see and to hear him. In these crowds were people of all political tendencies, but it made no difference if they were Republicans, Democrats, or Populists, all were equally glad to greet the President of the United States and the hero of San Juan Hill.

On this trip he frequently met some of the Rough Riders, and they invariably did all in their power to make him feel at home. On the other hand he showed that he had not forgotten them.

"By George, I am glad to see you!" he would exclaim, catching an old comrade by the hand. And his tone of voice would show that he meant just what he said.

For a long time the people of St. Louis had been preparing for a grand fair, to be known as the Louisiana Purchase Exposition, to commemorate the purchasing from France of all that vast territory of the United States which lies between the Mississippi River and the Rocky Mountains and the Gulf of Mexico and British America. The purchase was made in 1803 for fifteen millions of dollars, and it was hoped to hold the exposition on the one hundredth anniversary, in 1903, but matters were delayed, and so the fair was postponed until 1904.

The dedication of the fair buildings at the Exposition Grounds was held on April 30, 1903, and was made a gala occasion by those interested. President Roosevelt was invited to speak, and also Ex-President Cleveland, and both made addresses of remarkable interest. Following the dedication exercises a grand banquet was given at which the scene of good-fellowship was one not readily forgotten. The President wished the exposition well, and promised to do all in his power to make it a success.

Although the President had already travelled many miles, the greater part of his western trip still lay before him.

From St. Louis he went to Kansas City and to Topeka, where the citizens were as anxious to meet him as anywhere. He stopped at Sharon Springs over Sunday, and then went to Denver, and to various towns in Colorado and in New Mexico. While in New Mexico he became interested in the systems of irrigation there, and told the people what they might do if their systems of watering the ground were increased.

Having passed through the Grand Cañon, the second week in May found him in southern California. He visited Los Angeles, reviewing the annual floral parade, and many other points, and at Claremont addressed a great gathering of school children in a beautiful park filled with shrubs and flowers. The children were decidedly enthusiastic over the meeting, and when Mr. Roosevelt went away, some pelted him with flowers, which bombardment he took in good part.

President Roosevelt's visit to Leland Stanford Jr. University in California came next, and here the students cheered him with vigor. He visited many of the more important buildings, and was entertained by members of the faculty.

His face was now set toward the Golden Gate, and San Francisco was all alive to give him an ovation. It was his first official visit to the Pacific coast, and all whom he met vied with each other to do him honor, while they listened with great attention to what he had to say.

Three days were spent in San Francisco and vicinity, and three days more in a tour of the Yosemite Valley. President Roosevelt was particularly anxious to see some of the big trees of the State, and was driven to several that are well known.

The steps of the Chief Magistrate were now turned northward, to Oregon, and a week was spent at Portland, and in the towns and cities of the Puget Sound territory, and beyond. Here he saw much that was new and novel in the lumber trade and in the salmon industry, and was received with a warmth that could not be mistaken.

"He is a President for the whole country, no mistake about that," said more than one.

"He makes you feel he is your friend the minute you lay eyes on him," would put in another. To many in this far corner of our country, this visit of the President will ever remain as a pleasant memory. They could never hope to get to Washington, more than three thousand miles away, and to have him come out to see them was worth remembering.

The journey eastward was made through Montana to Salt Lake City and then to Cheyenne, where additional addresses were delivered. From the latter point a fast train bore him homeward, and by the next Sunday he was back in the White House once more, as fresh and hearty as ever, and well prepared to undertake whatever important work might come to hand.

And work was there in plenty. Among the first things taken up by the President was a scandal in the Post-Office Department. Without loss of time President Roosevelt ordered Postmaster General Payne to make a thorough investigation, with the result that many contracts which were harmful to our post-office system were annulled, and some wrong-doers were brought to justice.

Toward the end of July there was considerable disturbance in the Government Printing Office at Washington because a certain assistant foreman, who had been discharged, was reinstated. All of the bookbinders were on the point of striking because they did not want the man returned, as he did not belong to their union. But President Roosevelt was firm in the matter; and in the end the man went back, and there was no strike. This affair caused an almost endless discussion in labor circles, some claiming that the union should have been upheld, while others thought differently.

During the summer, as was his usual habit, President Roosevelt, with his family, spent part of his time at his country home at Oyster Bay. This time the visit to the old homestead was of unusual interest, for, on August 17, the North Atlantic Fleet of the navy visited that vicinity, for review and inspection by the President.

It was a gala occasion, and the fleet presented a handsome appearance as it filed past and thundered out a Presidential salute. Many distinguished guests were present, and all without exception spoke of the steady improvement in our navy as a whole. President Roosevelt was equally enthusiastic, and well he might be, for he had used every means in his power to make our navy all it should be.

Late in September President Roosevelt returned to Washington, and on October 15 delivered the principal address at the unveiling of a statue of that grand military hero, General Sherman. Here once more he was listened to with tremendous interest, delivering a speech that was patriotic to the core and full of inspiration.

For some time past matters in Colombia had been in a very mixed-up condition. The United States were willing to take hold of the Panama Canal, as already mentioned, but although a treaty had been made to that effect, the Colombian government would not ratify the agreement.

On November 3, the trouble in Colombia reached its culminating point. On that day the State of Panama declared itself free and independent. The people of that State wanted the canal built by the United States, and were very angry when the rest of the Colombian States would not agree to the treaty which had been made.

At once there were strong rumors of war, and a few slight attacks were really made. The United States forbade the transportation of soldiers on the Panama railroad, and a few days later recognized Panama as an independent republic. The new republic was likewise recognized by France, and, later still, by England. On November 9, Panama appointed a commission to negotiate a canal treaty with our country, and this treaty was signed and sealed at Washington by Secretary of State Hay, acting for the United States, and M. Bunau-Varilla, acting for Panama.

The President's next message to Congress went at great length into the question of the Panama Canal, and in defence of the recognition of the new republic. It also told of what the new Department of Commerce and Labor had accomplished, especially the branch devoted to corporations.

PRESIDENT ROOSEVELT SPEAKING AT THE UNVEILING OF THE STATUE OF GENERAL SHERMAN.
(*Photograph by Clinedinst, Washington, D.C.*)

"We need not be over-sensitive about the welfare of corporations which shrink from the light," wrote Mr. Roosevelt. And in this statement every one who had the best interests of our nation at heart agreed. To accomplish great works great corporations are often necessary, but they must conduct business in such a fashion that they are not ashamed to show their methods to the public at large.

At the opening of the year 1904 there were strong rumors of a war between Japan and Russia, over the occupation of Korea, and this war started early in February by a battle on the sea, wherein the Russian fleet lost several war-ships. This contest was followed by others of more or less importance, and it looked as if, sooner or later, other nations might become involved in the struggle.

"We must keep our hands off," said President Roosevelt, and at once issued a proclamation, calling on all good citizens to remain strictly neutral, and warning those who might take part that they could hope for no aid from the United States should they get into trouble personally or have any property confiscated. This proclamation was followed by some excellent work of our State Department, whereby it was agreed among the leading nations that the zone of fighting should be a limited one, that is, that neither Japan nor Russia should be allowed to carry it beyond a certain defined territory.

For many weeks Congress had debated the Panama Canal treaty and the action of President Roosevelt regarding the new republic of Panama. On February 23, 1904, a vote was taken in the Senate, and the Panama Canal treaty was ratified in all particulars. Without delay some United States troops were despatched to Panama, to guard the strip of land ten miles wide through which the canal is to run, and preparations were made to push the work on the waterway without further delay.

On Saturday, April 30, the great World's Fair at St. Louis was formally opened to the public. It had cost over fifty millions of dollars and was designed to eclipse any fair held in the past. The opening was attended by two hundred thousand visitors, all of whom were more than pleased with everything to be seen.

It had been arranged that President Roosevelt should formally open the Exposition by means of telegraphic communications from the White House to the fair grounds. A key of ivory and gold was used for the purpose, and as soon as it was touched a salute of twenty-one guns roared forth in the Exposition's honor. Around the President were assembled the members of his Cabinet and representatives of many foreign nations. Before touching the key which was to set the machinery of the wonderful fair in motion, President Roosevelt spoke as follows:

"I have received from the Exposition grounds the statement that the management of the Louisiana Purchase Exposition awaits the pressing of the button which is to transmit the electric energy which is to unfurl the flag and start the machinery of the Exposition.

"I wish now to greet all present, and especially the representatives of the foreign nations here represented, in the name of the American people, and to thank these representatives for the parts their several countries have taken in being represented in this centennial anniversary of the greatest step in the movement which transformed the American Republic from a small confederacy of States lying along the Atlantic seaboard into a continental nation.

"This Exposition is one primarily intended to show the progress in the industry, the science, and the art, not only of the American nation, but of all other nations, in the great and wonderful century which has just closed. Every department of human activity will be represented there, and perhaps I may be allowed, as honorary president of the athletic association which, under European management, started to revive the memory of the Olympic games, to say that I am glad that, in addition to paying proper heed to the progress of industry, of science, of art, we have also paid proper heed to the development of the athletic pastimes which are useful in themselves as showing that it is wise for nations to be able to relax.

"I greet you all. I appreciate your having come here on this occasion, and in the presence of you, representing the American government and the governments of the foreign nations, I here open the Louisiana Exposition."

CHAPTER XXX

PERSONAL CHARACTERISTICS OF THEODORE ROOSEVELT THE PRESIDENT'S FAMILY LIFE AT THE WHITE HOUSE OUR COUNTRY AND ITS FUTURE

In reading over the foregoing pages the question may occur to some of my young readers, How is it possible for President Roosevelt to accomplish so much and still have time in which to occasionally enjoy himself by travelling or by going on a hunting tour?

The answer is a very simple one. Mr. Roosevelt works systematically, as do all who want their labor to amount to something. Years ago, when he was physically weak, he determined to make himself strong. He persisted in vigorous exercise, especially in the open air, and in the end attained a bodily health which any ordinary man may well envy.

The President does each day's work as it comes before him. He does not borrow trouble or cross a bridge before he comes to it. Whatever there is to do he does to the very best of his ability, and he allows future complications to take care of themselves. If a mistake is made, he does not worry continually over it, but keeps it in mind, so that a like mistake shall not occur again. When once his hand is on the plough, he does not believe in turning back. He has unlimited faith in the future of our glorious country, and a like faith in the honor and courage of his fellow-citizens.

Any man to be an intelligent worker cannot be dissipated, and the President is a good illustration of this. He has a good appetite, but eats moderately, and does not depend upon stimulants or tobacco to "brace him up" when the work is extra heavy. He goes out nearly every day for a walk, a ride on horseback, or a drive with some members of his family, and as a result of this, when night comes, sleeps soundly and arises the next morning as bright and fresh as ever.

This is the first time that a President with a large family has occupied the White House. Other Presidents have had a few children, but Mr. Roosevelt took possession with six, a hearty, romping crowd, the younger members of which thought it great fun to explore the executive mansion when first they moved in. The President loves his children dearly, and is not above "playing bear" with the little ones when time permits and they want some fun.

Of Mrs. Roosevelt it can truthfully be said that she makes a splendid "first lady in the land." She takes a great interest in all social functions, and an equal interest in what is best for her boys and girls and their friends. She is very charitable, and each year contributes liberally to hundreds of bazaars and fairs held throughout our country.

The oldest child of the President is Miss Alice Lee Roosevelt, named after her mother, the first wife of the Chief Magistrate. Although but a step-daughter to the present Mrs. Roosevelt, the two are as intimate and loving as if of the same flesh and blood. Miss Roosevelt has already made her debut in Washington society, and assisted at several gatherings at the White House.

All of the other children were born after Mr. Roosevelt's second marriage. His oldest son is Theodore Roosevelt, Jr., commonly called by his chums, Teddy, Jr. He is a lad of sixteen, bright and clever, and has been attending a college preparatory school at Groton, Massachusetts, as already mentioned. He loves outdoor games, and is said to possess many tastes in common with his father.

The other members of the family are, Kermit, fourteen, Ethel Carew, twelve, Archibald Bullock, nine, and a lively little boy named Quentin, who is six.

Some time ago a distinguished member of the English Educational Commission visited this country and made an inspection of our school system. When asked what had impressed him most deeply, he answered:

"The children of the President of the United States sitting side by side with the children of your workingmen in the public schools."

This simple little speech speaks volumes for the good, hard common sense of our President. He believes thoroughly in our public institutions, and knows the real value of sending out his boys to fight their own battles in the world at large. He does not believe in pampering children, but in making them self-reliant. All love to go out with him, and when at Oyster Bay he frequently takes the boys and their cousins for a day's tramp through the woods or along the beach, or else for a good hard row on the bay. The President prefers rowing to sailing, and frequently rows for several miles at a stretch. His enjoyment of bathing is as great as ever, and his boys love to go into the water with him.

Christmas time at the White House is just as full of joy there as it is anywhere. The younger children hang up their stockings, and scream with delight over every new toy received. For some days previous to Christmas one of the rooms is turned into a storeroom, and to this only Mrs. Roosevelt and one of the maids hold the key. Presents come in from everywhere, including many for the President, for his friends far and near insist upon remembering him. These presents are arranged on a large oval table near one of the broad windows, and on Christmas morning the distribution begins.

The President, in his trips to the woods, has seen the great harm done by cutting down promising evergreens, so he does not believe very much in having a Christmas tree. But a year ago a great surprise awaited him.

"I'm going to fix up a tree," said little Archie, and managed to smuggle a small evergreen into the house and place it in a large closet that was not being used. Here he and his younger brother Quentin worked for several days in arranging the tree just to suit them. On Christmas morning, after the presents were given out, both asked their father to come to where the closet was located.

"What is up now?" asked Mr. Roosevelt, curiously.

"Come and see!" they shouted. And he went, followed by all the others of the family. Then the closet door was thrown open, and there stood the tree, blazing with lights. It was certainly a great surprise, and Mr. Roosevelt enjoyed it as much as anybody.

The children of Washington, and especially those whose fathers occupy public positions, always look forward with anticipations of great pleasure to the children's parties given by Mrs. Roosevelt, and these parties are of equal interest to those living at the mansion.

PRESIDENT ROOSEVELT AND HIS FAMILY.
(*Photograph by Pach Bros., N.Y.*)

Such a party was given during the last holidays, and was attended by several hundred children, all of whom, of course, came arrayed in their best. They were received by Mrs. Roosevelt, who had a hand-shake and a kind word for each, and then some of the Cabinet ladies, who were assisting, gave to each visitor a button, set in ribbon and tinsel and inscribed "Merry Christmas and Happy New Year."

The big main dining-room of the White House had been prepared for the occasion. There was a Christmas tree at one side of the room, and the table was filled with fruit, cake, and candy. The President came in and helped to pass the ice-cream and cake, and Theodore, Jr. and some of the others passed the candy and other good things.

After this the visitors were asked to go to the East Room and dance. The Marine Band furnished the music, and while the children were dancing, the President came in to look at them. The entertainment lasted until the end of the afternoon, and when the visitors departed, President Roosevelt was at the door to shake hands and bid them good-by.

And here let us bid good-by ourselves, wishing Theodore Roosevelt and his family well. What the future holds in store for our President no man can tell. That he richly deserves the honors that have come to him, is beyond question. He has done his best to place and keep our United States in the front rank of the nations of the world. Under him, as under President McKinley, progress has been remarkably rapid. In the uttermost parts of the world our Flag is respected as it was never respected before. Perhaps some few mistakes have been made, but on the whole our advancement has been justified, and is eminently satisfactory. The future is large with possibilities, and it remains for the generation I am addressing to rise up and embrace those opportunities and make the most of them.

APPENDIX A

BRIEF EXTRACTS FROM FAMOUS ADDRESSES DELIVERED BY THEODORE ROOSEVELT

"If we are to be a really great people, we must strive in good faith to play a great part in the world. We cannot avoid meeting great issues. All that we can determine for ourselves is whether we shall meet them well or ill."

"All honor must be paid to the architects of our material prosperity; to the captains of industry who have built our factories and our railroads; to the strong men who toil for wealth with brain or hand; for great is the debt of the nation to these and their kind. But our debt is still greater to the men whose highest type is to be found in a statesman like Lincoln, a soldier like Grant."

"A man's first duty is to his own home, but he is not thereby excused from doing his duty to the state; for if he fails in this second duty it is under the penalty of ceasing to be a freeman."

Extracts from "The Strenuous Life."

"Is America a weakling to shrink from the work that must be done by the world's powers? No! The young giant of the West stands on a continent and clasps the crest of an ocean in either hand. Our nation, glorious in youth and strength, looks into the future with eager and fearless eyes, and rejoices, as a strong man to run the race."

Extract from Speech seconding the Nomination of William McKinley for President.

"Poverty is a bitter thing, but it is not as bitter as the existence of restless vacuity and physical, moral, and intellectual flabbiness to which those doom themselves who elect to spend all their years in that vainest of all vain pursuits, the pursuit of mere pleasure."

"Our interests are at bottom common; in the long run we go up or go down together."

"The first essential of civilization is law. Anarchy is simply the hand-maiden and forerunner of tyranny and despotism. Law and order, enforced by justice and by strength, lie at the foundation of civilization."

Extracts from a Speech delivered at Minneapolis, Minnesota, September 2, 1901.

"We hold work, not as a curse, but as a blessing, and we regard the idler with scornful pity."

"Each man must choose, so far as the conditions allow him, the path to which he is bidden by his own peculiar powers and inclinations. But if he is a man, he must in some way or shape do a man's work."

"It is not given to us all to succeed, but it is given to us all to strive manfully to deserve success."

"We cannot retain the full measure of our self-respect if we do not retain pride in our citizenship."

Extracts from an Address on "Manhood and Statehood."

"The true welfare of the nation is indissolubly bound up in the welfare of the farmer and wage-worker; of the man who tills the soil, and of the mechanic, the handicraftsman, and the laborer. The poorest motto upon which an American can act is the motto of 'some men down,' and the safest to follow is that of 'all men up.'"

Extract from Speech delivered at the Dedication of the Pan-American Fair Buildings.

"The men we need are the men of strong, earnest, solid character the men who possess the homely virtues, and who to these virtues add rugged courage, rugged honesty, and high resolve."

Extract from Speech delivered upon the Life of General Grant.

APPENDIX B

LIST OF THEODORE ROOSEVELT'S WRITINGS

Books:

The Naval War of 1812, 2 volumes. (1882.)
The Winning of the West, 6 volumes. (1889-1896.)
Hunting Trips of a Ranchman. (1885.)
Hunting Trips on the Prairie. (Companion volume to that above. 1885.)
The Wilderness Hunter. (1893.)
Hunting the Grisly. (Companion volume to that above. 1893.)
The Rough Riders. (1899.)
Life of Oliver Cromwell. (1900.)
The Strenuous Life Essays and Addresses. (1900.)
American Ideals. (1897.)
Administration Civil Service. (1898.)
Life of Thomas Hart Benton. (1887.)
New York. (Historic Towns Series. 1891.)
Life of Gouverneur Morris. (1888.)
Ranch Life and the Hunting Trail. (1888.)
Essays on Practical Politics. (1888.)

Written by Theodore Roosevelt and Henry Cabot Lodge:

Hero Tales from American History. (1895.)

Written by Theodore Roosevelt and G.B. Grinnell:

Trail and Camp Fire. (1896.)
Hunting in Many Lands. (1896.)

Principal Magazine Articles:

Admiral Dewey. (McClure's Magazine.)
Military Preparedness and Unpreparedness. (Century Magazine.)
Mad Anthony Wayne's Victory. (Harper's Magazine.)

St. Clair's Defeat. (Harper's Magazine.)
Fights between Iron Clads. (Century Magazine.)
Need of a New Navy. (Review of Reviews.)

APPENDIX C

CHRONOLOGY OF THE LIFE OF THEODORE ROOSEVELT FROM 1858 TO 1904

1858. October 27. Theodore Roosevelt born in New York City, son of Theodore Roosevelt and Martha (Bullock) Roosevelt.

1864. Sent to public school, and also received some private instruction; spent summers at Oyster Bay, New York.

1873. Became a member of the Dutch Reformed Church; has been a member ever since.

1876. September. Entered Harvard College. Member of numerous clubs and societies.

1878. February 9. Death of Theodore Roosevelt, Sr.

1880. June. Graduated from Harvard College; a Phi Beta Kappa man.
September 23. Married Miss Alice Lee, of Boston, Massachusetts.
Travelled extensively in Europe; climbed the Alps; made a member of the Alpine Club of London.

1881. Elected a member of the New York Assembly, and served for three terms in succession.

1884. Birth of daughter, Alice Lee Roosevelt.
Death of Mrs. Alice (Lee) Roosevelt, Mr. Roosevelt's first wife.
Death of Mrs. Martha (Bullock) Roosevelt, Mr. Roosevelt's mother.
Made Delegate-at-large to the Republican National Convention that nominated James G. Blaine for President.

1885. Became a ranchman and hunter.

1886. Ran for office of mayor of New York City, and was defeated by Abram Hewitt.
Spent additional time in hunting.
December 2. Married Edith Kermit Carew, of New York City.

1888. Birth of son, Theodore Roosevelt, Jr.
September. Grand hunt in the Selkirk Mountains.

1889. May. Appointed by President Harrison a member of the Civil Service Commission; served for six years, four under
President Harrison and two under President Cleveland.

1890. Birth of son, Kermit Roosevelt.

1891. September. Grand hunt at Two-Ocean Pass, Wyoming.

1892. Birth of daughter, Ethel Carew Roosevelt.

1895. May 24. Appointed Police Commissioner of New York City by Mayor William Strong. Served until April, 1897.
Birth of son, Archibald Bullock Roosevelt.

1897. April. Made First Assistant Secretary of the Navy, under Secretary Long and President McKinley.
Birth of son, Quentin Roosevelt.

1898. April 25. Congress declared war with Spain. Roosevelt

resigned his position in the Navy Department.
May. Helped to organize the Rough Riders, and was appointed Lieutenant-Colonel, May 6.
May 29. The Rough Riders left San Antonio, Texas, for Tampa, Florida.
June 2. In camp at Tampa.
June 7. Move by coal cars to Port Tampa; four companies left behind; board transport *Yucatan*.
June 13. Start for Cuba, without horses.
June 22. Landing of the Rough Riders at Daiquiri.
June 23. March to Siboney.
June 24. Advance to La Guasima (Las Guasimas). First fight with the Spanish troops.
July 1. Battles of San Juan and El Caney. Roosevelt leads the Rough Riders up San Juan Hill.
July 2. Fighting in the trenches by the Rough Riders, Roosevelt in command.
July 3. Sinking of the Spanish fleet off Santiago Bay.
July 8. Roosevelt made Colonel of the Rough Riders.
August 7. Departure of the Rough Riders from Cuba.
August 9. Spain accepts terms of peace offered by the United States.
August 16. Arrival of the Rough Riders at Montauk, Long Island.
September 15. Mustering out of the Rough Riders.
September 27. Nominated by the Republican party for governor of New York.
October. Grand campaigning tour through the Empire State.
November. Elected governor of New York by seventeen thousand plurality.

1899. January 1. Assumed office as governor of New York.
April 10. Delivered famous address on "The Strenuous Life,"

at Chicago.

September 29 and 30. Governor appointed these days as holidays in honor of a reception to Admiral Dewey; grand water and land processions.

1900. June 19. Republican Convention met at Philadelphia; Roosevelt seconded the nomination of McKinley for President (second term), and was nominated for the Vice-Presidency.

July, August, and September. Governor Roosevelt travelled 20,000 miles, delivering 673 political speeches. at nearly 600 cities and towns.

November 6. McKinley and Roosevelt carried 28 states, Democratic opponents carried 17 states; Republican electoral votes, 292, Democratic and scattering combined, 155.

December. Presided over one short session of the United States Senate.

1901. January 11. Started on a five weeks' hunting tour in Northwest Colorado; bringing down many cougars.

April. Attended the dedication of the Pan-American Exposition buildings at Buffalo, New York, and delivered an address.

September 6. Received word, while at Isle la Motte, Vermont, that President McKinley had been shot; hurried at once to Buffalo; assured that the President would recover, joined his family in the Adirondacks.

September 14. Death of President McKinley. Roosevelt returned to Buffalo; took the oath of office as President of the United States at the house of Ansley Wilcox; retained the McKinley Cabinet.

September 15 to 19. Funeral of President McKinley, at Buffalo, Washington, and Canton, Ohio.
President Roosevelt attended.
September 20. First regular working day of President Roosevelt at the White House.
December 3. First annual message delivered to Congress.
December 4. Senate received Hay-Pauncefote canal treaty from the President.
December 17. First break in the McKinley Cabinet. Postmaster General Smith resigned; was succeeded by H.C. Payne.

1902. January 3. Grand ball at the White House, Miss Alice Roosevelt formally presented to Washington society.
January 6. Secretary Gage of the Treasury resigned; was succeeded by Ex-Governor Leslie M. Shaw, of Iowa.
January 20. The President transmitted to Congress report of Canal Commission, recommending buying
of rights for $40,000,000.
February 10. Serious sickness of Theodore Roosevelt, Jr. President in attendance at Groton, Massachusetts, several days.
February 24. Reception to Prince Henry of Prussia.
February 25. Launching of German Emperor's yacht, which was christened by Miss Alice Roosevelt.
March 7. President signed a bill creating a permanent pension bureau.
May 12. Beginning of the great coal strike; largest in the history of the United States.
May 21. President unveiled a monument at Arlington Cemetery, erected in memory of those
who fell in the Spanish-American War.
June 9. President reviewed West Point cadets at the

centennial celebration of that institution.
July 4. Addressed a great gathering at Pittsburg.
July 5. Removed his business offices to Oyster Bay for the summer.
August 11. Retirement of Justice Gray of the Supreme Court; the President named Oliver Wendell Holmes
as his successor.
August 22. The President began a twelve days' tour of New England.
September 3. Narrow escape from death near Pittsfield, Massachusetts. Trolley car ran down carriage,
killing Secret Service attendant.
September 6 and 7. President visited Chattanooga, Tennessee, and delivered addresses.
October 3. President called conference at Washington concerning coal strike.
October 21. As a result of several meetings between the President, the mine operators, and the mine workers
the miners resumed work, and a commission was appointed by the President to adjust matters in dispute.
November 19. Grand reception to the President at Memphis, Tennessee.
December 2. President's message to Congress was read by both branches.

1903. January 15. President signed the free coal bill passed by Congress.
January 21. President signed the bill for the reorganization of the military system.
March 5. Special session of Congress called by the President to consider Cuban reciprocity bill and
Panama Canal treaty with Colombia.
March 12. President appointed a Commission to report on

organization, needs, and conditions of government work.

March 18. President received report of Coal Commission.

April 2. President received degree of LL.D. from the University of Chicago. Beginning of long trip to the west.

April 4. President addressed Minnesota legislature at St. Paul.

April 30. President delivered address at dedication of buildings of the Louisiana Purchase Exposition, at St. Louis.

June 6. President ordered an investigation into the Post-office Department scandals.

July 4. First message around the world, via new Pacific cable, received by President at Oyster Bay.

July 23. The President refused to consider charges made by a bookbinders' union against a workman in the Government Printing Office, thereby declaring for an "open" shop.

August 17. Grand naval review by the President, on Long Island Sound, near Oyster Bay.

September 17. President delivered an address at the dedication of a monument to New Jersey soldiers, on the battle-field of Antietam.

October 15. President delivered an address at unveiling of statue to General Sherman, at Washington.

October 20. President called extra session of Congress to consider a commercial treaty with Cuba.

November 3. Panama proclaimed independent of Colombia.

November 6. The United States government formally recognized the independence of the state of Panama.

November 10. Opening of extra session of Congress called by President to consider commercial treaty with Cuba.

November 18. A new canal treaty was formally signed at Washington by Secretary Hay, of the United States, and M. Bunau-Varilla, acting for

Panama.

December 2. The canal treaty was ratified at Panama.

December 7. The President sent regular message to Congress especially defending the administration policy regarding Panama and the canal.

1904. January 4. The President sent a special message to Congress regarding the recognition of the new republic of Panama. This was followed for weeks by debates, for and against the action of the administration.

February. War broke out between Japan and Russia; the President issued a proclamation declaring the neutrality of the United States.

February 22. The President and family assisted at a Washington's Birthday tree-planting at the White House grounds.

February 23. The United States ratified all the provisions of the Panama Canal treaty; preparations were made, under the directions of the President, to begin work without delay.

April 30. President, at Washington, delivered address and pressed telegraphic key opening World's Fair at St. Louis.

---

[1] For other extracts from this speech, see Appendix A, p. 297.

[2] See "American Boys' Life of William McKinley," p. 191.

[3] For this speech in full, and for what happened after it was delivered, see "American Boys' Life of McKinley."

www.ingramcontent.com/pod-product-compliance
Lightning Source LLC
Chambersburg PA
CBHW052113200426
43209CB00057B/1603